NEVER
NEVER
LAND

NEVER NEVER LAND

A Novel

Namita Gokhale

SPEAKING TIGER

SPEAKING TIGER BOOKS LLP
125A, Ground Floor, Shahpur Jat, near Asiad Village,
New Delhi 110049

First published by Speaking Tiger Books in 2024

ISBN: 978-93-5447-704-1
eISBN: 978-93-5447-705-8

10 9 8 7 6 5 4 3 2 1

Typeset in Arno Pro by SÜRYA, New Delhi
Printed at Chaman Enterprises, New Delhi

'The prospect of death is what gives life the whole of its piquancy. Life would be so much more pointless if there were no feeling that it must end.'

—Muriel Spark, in an interview given in 1959
to mark the publication of her novel *Memento Mori*

'It is like wartime,' Miss Taylor remarked.

'What do you say?'

'Being over seventy is like being engaged in a war. All our friends are going or gone and we survive among the dead and the dying as on a battlefield.'

—Muriel Spark, *Memento Mori*

‘It’s sad but not sad we love the darkness
Ghosts—who let you in? I swore
I locked the door. Even those who can’t touch
drink wine together as the moon rises.’

—@KelliAgodon, waxwingmag.org

CONTENTS

1. LEAVING

The sky is a grey rag, and the air toxic and always muggy. The Delhi monsoon is a betrayal. There was a time, I'm told, when gentle black mammoths poured down relief from the sky and the city was damp and cool for weeks. Everything washed clean. Love and heady things like that seemed to be round the corner. That hasn't been my experience.

Moving to Gurgaon—I can never call it Gurugram—has made the scars of the betrayal multiply. I live alone, in a rented room just beyond Cyber City. I'm on the third floor, in a house without a lift. I see no trees from my window, only grey sky and glass towers that hurt the eye. My landlady loves dogs. The front entrance has a permanent smell of sour milk and stale bread. But my room is nice—I've made it nice—and the WiFi connection is good.

My LinkedIn profile says 'Freelance Editor', after I lost my job this summer, when South Pole Books decided to shut down their India office. I proofread manuscripts now, sometimes copy edit them, and take up small writing gigs that turn up. I'm trying to write a novel. I read. I'm lonely. Frankly, I'm a wreck.

I lurk on the edges of my school WhatsApp group. Our batch. The class of 1982, St Dolorosa Convent. It was actually the Mater Dolorosa Convent when I studied there. Our Lady of Sorrows. They changed the name to St Dolorosa the year after we passed out, and then, eight years ago, they made it co-educational. They raised the fees. They built an indoor stadium.

My schoolmates don't seem to have a care in the world. They babble incessantly about their children, their holidays abroad (less so after the pandemic), and inane forwards that seem factually unsubstantiated (not that they care).

Trad wives living trad lives. Family photographs.

Videos. The children, the grandchildren, lush gardens for those who have them. Pets and nieces and nephews for grade two lives. Obituaries sometimes, of siblings, parents, pets. Crying face emojis, a yellow face with raised eyebrows and a slight frown shedding a single, blue tear from one eye. Or a heartbreak emoticon. Boo hoo.

Their lives stink of safety and leisure and the security nets of family. They post pictures of their houses and vacations. Yet they are kind, and concerned about each other. They inhabit real lives. They are not shadows. Do they know this pointless, bitter anger, this bile that inhabits me?

I haven't physically encountered any of them for years, or indeed, decades. How many years since we had our graduation party? 'Let's all meet twenty-five years later,' I had said to my best friend, or rather my only friend, Anita Shivdasani. She had giggled, and a sliver of spit had fallen from her lips to mine. I hadn't minded.

We hadn't met after that as her parents had moved to America. She sent me a couple of postcards, and then she killed herself the morning she turned twenty-five. Her mother had written me a letter from Denver, asking me to send her any photographs I might have of her daughter. I sent her the only one I had. Anita and I in the school playground, holding a little chalice, the size of our palms. We had finished second in the three-legged race. We were in the seventh grade.

Those girls of '82, they share jokes on the group, and puzzles, and credulity-straining forwards. Most of them seem to exist in plurals and multiples—it's a virtual Noah's Ark, with the animals walking in two by two. But there's also Aruna who is widowed, and Anahita who never married, and Sita and Sunita, the bohemian Bhalla sisters, who seem to have moved to Australia. It's a group of about forty-five women, all in their mid-fifties, like me.

Last week, there was this message from the group administrator, Daya Vaswani. 'Hey girls,' she blared, as though from a megaphone. 'Some of you never seem to respond, to reply, to be part of the group. No likes, no reactions, no hearts or emojis. Sita, Sunita, Iti, Renu, Piya, Sarita, you seem to have disappeared from our group. I was scrolling through to see the status of our members, and you seem silent and disinterested. Please connect with us within this week. Otherwise, it's best you drop out and leave the group.'

It was a bolt from the blue. I couldn't leave the group. I wouldn't leave the group. In a way, they were all I had, my link with myself. It was thoughtless of Daya, cruel of her to send out that message. She was whipping us. Well, I wouldn't yelp. I would reply, and crawl back into the group. They were my virtual family, my mirror to myself.

I decided to wait for a day before I replied. It was a weekend, and I returned to the manuscript I was working on. It was a senseless, tasteless piece of writing, but, or perhaps therefore, I was being paid a lot to clean it up.

The milk had gone sour and the coffee I made for myself tasted like puke. I soldiered on, correcting spellings and tenses, connecting the disconnects, joining the dots. It was yet another thinly disguised autobiographical novel, written with heartbreak without heart, and courage that did not ring true. I could write better than that. Then why didn't I?

I replied to the ultimatum on Monday. 'Hello Daya! Good morning girls!! Sorry I had gone silent, it's been a busy time and I was caught up. Promise regular updates from now!'

Then I returned to the other problems of the present. No milk. I would go vegan. No work. I would submit *Promises to Myself* to the literary agency that had commissioned the novel. It was a miserable first draft I had somehow cobbled together. It didn't work, I knew as an editor that it didn't work, but I would send it to the agency anyway. Lots of terrible books were published and some of them were successes.

I would email the two publishing houses who seemed to want my services to check if they wanted me to work on some more copy editing. I'm a good editor—I'm not diffident about saying that. It's just when I get to my own creative writing that it gets messy and spills all over the page.

I would work on my new novel. It's called *HypeReality*. That's only tentative, a working title. What's it about? I don't know, I really can't say. I don't want to discuss it, I'll say to the literary agent. Not yet. Let the story develop—or the lack of a story, I think, but won't tell him. He has grown big enough to drop me and move on.

I'm not sure of anything anymore. Gurgaon doesn't let me feel the ground beneath my feet. And it's not even modern and urban, just a dusty, sludgy, vertical slum. At least the bit of it where I am suspended is. For Meta or for verse.

I breathe filtered air, and all my connections are virtual. No harm in that, it's better than the 'real' thing, but disorienting, somehow, somewhere. There will come a day when I'll lock myself in and never go out. They'll have to break open the door, handkerchiefs tied over nose and mouth for the smell of piss and shit or death. It can happen to anyone, we all walk a thin line.

Should I leave? How should I leave? Where should I go?

It came to me that night. The call of home. I dreamt of the mountains, of jagged pines and blue skies and the whispering wind. I woke up the next morning, packed my bags, and set off for Kumaon. For The Dacha. Where everything began.

2. THE CALL OF THE MOUNTAINS

A girl. A woman. An old woman. Two old women. The cold mountain air. The rain and the damp. The shifting earth.

She returned to the Himalaya, The Abode of Snow. It was August, the rivers were in spate, and the mountains were defiantly hurling rocks at the newly built highways. The long Independence Day weekend was upon them, and cars were crawling up the rain-sodden hills in single files, with people running away. Or running back, seeking sanctuary amidst the mist and the fog. Among this latter lot, Iti Arya, visiting her grandmother at The Dacha, her village home.

When she was young, Iti had heard the mountains speak—or so she'd imagined. They would circle her like wise old men with long beards and say things to her. 'Listen to us,' they would bend low and whisper. 'We are there for you, through rain and sleet, through rain and snow. Don't be afraid.'

'What about the sunny days, and the summer months?' she had asked, her eyes alight with wonder.

One of the mountains had stroked his beard thoughtfully. 'The Sun has his own stories,' he had replied, 'and his own ways of telling them. You can hear him best at mid-day, when he casts no shadows.'

Iti had told her grandmother about her encounter with the wise men. Badi Amma had listened impassively, and then nodded. 'You must listen carefully when the mountains speak to you,' she had said, stroking Iti's plump cheeks. 'They don't speak to everybody. And don't tell your mother of this, she won't understand. No need to tell everybody everything.'

Iti told her grandmother everything in those faraway days. Her grandmother was ninety now. Perhaps more. She lived with her erstwhile employer. Her village home, about an hour's walk away, in Khata Khumani, was securely padlocked. Her two cows, Gori and Gaurali, had been entrusted to her nearest neighbours, who lived some distance away.

The taxi drove up a steep hill and dropped her off at Rosinka's cottage. She remembered it as a grainy long-ago memory, but nothing had prepared her for the sight that she encountered.

The rain stopped and the sun broke out. The light was translucent, and raindrops trembled like festive fairy lights along the pebbled path. Iti forgot about the taxi, and Badi Amma, and settled down on a low wooden bench that seemed placed in the garden just for her. Clouds floated through the valley below, and a veil of mist danced across the middle distance. And in the sky, a double rainbow, greeting her, welcoming her, telling her she was home.

The taxi driver, a young lad from Haryana, looked around and absorbed the beauty of his surroundings. He didn't disturb his passenger, who seemed to have gone into a trance.

An old lady walked up to greet her. There was a spring to her step. She was draped in a voluminous woollen shawl with ruffled edges. They embraced each other.

Another woman appeared. She walked slowly, cautiously, with the help of an aluminium walker. His passenger bent down to touch her feet.

The cabbie unloaded her baggage, which the woman seemed to have forgotten about, and deposited it in the verandah that skirted the house. A beautiful young girl came forward to give him a mug of tea. She had golden hair and blue eyes. He stared at her in fascination.

The taxi was a prepaid one. His passenger seemed in no mood to give him a tip. She signed the bill and smiled absently. He left. There was something strange about the place, he decided. It was ghosted—like a bhoot bangla.

That night, Iti wrote an account of her arrival in her journal.

My grandmother, Badi Amma, was quietly happy to see me. She didn't say much, but I could feel it in the gentle pressure of her chapped hands as she held me close. I hadn't seen her for almost a decade now. I had been running away from myself, and had abandoned and neglected her, but the years fell away with the touch of her work-worn hands.

Badi Amma had worked as a house-maid—cleaning, scrubbing, cooking. She inched up the hierarchy until she was slowly elevated to a sort of Pahadi lady-in-waiting for her mistress, Rosinka Paul Singh.

It used to embarrass, and even humiliate me, to think of my beloved grandmother as a convenience, a glorified house help. Yet when I look back now, I realise that it was as much a story of a complex friendship as of class and social order.

Rosinka is a hundred and two years old, robust, cheerful, and vain about her appearance. Badi Amma is younger—by ten years, or twelve, or eight. It is difficult to be certain. Rosinka calls her Lily. She was named Lila but Lily suited her mistress better. The pair of them have aged well, achieved a sort of timelessness that has them residing as much in memory as in the present.

Perhaps I should archive their memories. But I've just realised there is no connectivity here. My phone looks at me reproachfully. No social media. No email. Just silence, and the hooting of owls outside my window. I guess this journal will have to be my companion. There is a certain relief in returning to the pen, though the keyboard beckons.

Goodnight, dear diary. I shall keep you posted.

3. SUNSHINE AND SHADOWS

Her bedroom was up a narrow flight of stairs and had a balcony that overlooked the valley. Iti woke up to sunshine and a view of the snow peaks. Nanda Devi glittered in the distance, and then the panorama of the other heights. The respite from the monsoons didn't last long, and soon the rainclouds roiled over to obscure the snows. A slow drizzle settled over the garden. Iti went down in search of coffee.

A young girl with long straight hair bleached blonde, a Gen Z, was sitting in the kitchen poring over a book. She was the one who had brought tea for the cabbie when they arrived. Her blue eyes countered Iti's curious gaze. She greeted the visitor with calm composure. 'Good morning,' she said. 'I'm Nina. I'm Badi Amma's granddaughter.'

How could this be? Iti had been brought up to believe that her mother was the only child of the widowed Badi Amma. She didn't know of any cousins. Nina was lying, or deluded.

Iti masked her surprise. 'Then we must be cousins!' she said cheerily, bending forward to give Nina a kiss. The young girl drew back, and bit her lips. She continued chewing on them absent-mindedly.

Something about Nina irritated Iti viscerally. This was her home, Badi Amma was her grandmother. She resented the intrusion.

'I like your blonde hair,' she said cattily, 'but why are you wearing blue contact lenses? What's the scene?'

'Every emotion has a colour,' Nina replied neutrally. 'I'm feeling blue this week, and so that's how I represent myself. If I can fix my exterior, I can search my interior. It's about representation.'

Iti was momentarily stumped and realised afresh how much she hated the young. Smug, ignorant know-it-alls. She summoned all the spite coiled inside her. 'I hope you continue to have a blue weekend,' she said, unsmiling. Nina smiled back serenely.

Iti tried to recall the family tree. Badi Amma's husband had died when she was just nineteen. She continued to live in the slate-roofed cottage up the hill, and to work as day help for Rosinka, who had a great retinue of servants in those days.

Iti's mother had been a year old when she lost her father. Badi Amma's elder sister, also widowed, moved in and helped bring up the child. Rosinka kept an eye on the child, and saw to it that she learned to read and write. When Iti's mother turned nine, she had been dispatched to St Anne's, a missionary school in nearby Bhowali. She had then been sent to nursing college in Bareilly, where she met Iti's father, Shailesh Arya, a Garhwali from Dehradun, a salesman in a chemist's shop.

Iti could no longer clearly recall what her mother looked like. All she could remember was the hesitancy in her voice, the self-effacing step back wherever she might be, as if she did not want to be visible or present. What wound in her childhood could have done that to her, Iti wondered, a rare compassion rising in her heart as she thought of her mother.

4. RAIN IN THE MOUNTAINS

Who could Nina be? My mother did not have it in her to make a secret life. What I don't know about her I don't because I have never really wanted to know.

My mother had cut off from Badi Amma after her marriage. She had been deeply mortified by her mother's existence as a menial, a mere maid. But Rosinka had tenaciously continued to insist on my annual visits.

My memories of those trips to the hills are garbled into a long dream, sometimes a nightmare. Rosinka's hold over my mother ensured that she would take leave from her nursing home job in Roorkee to collect me from my school and drop me to The Dacha every summer. The house was called 'The Hideaway' in those days—that was the name Rosinka's husband Peter Paul Singh had given it.

Peter Paul Singh had died young, as had my grandfather. Nobody ever mentioned them after they left the world—it was as though they had never existed, the inheritor of a small fortune who painted, and the man who tilled half a bigha of terraced land twice a year. Rosinka and Lily continued with their lives. The house was renamed 'The Dacha' as a reminder of Rosinka's exalted Russian lineage. But the villagers got confused and began calling it 'Chacha', the name by which it is known to this day.

My father had died early on as well. No one knew how. It was rumoured that he had drowned in the Roorkee canal. There was a concurrent rumour that he had run away with a Tibetan woman and set up a momo stall in the border town of Mahendranagar. I was born a couple of months later in Khata Khumani. It was Badi Amma who brought me up, carrying me to The Dacha with her every day, till her sister arrived to look after me. My mother would come from Roorkee for a day or two every few months to look at me impassively. Her lower lip twitched when she had to hold or carry me. Perhaps I'm only imagining this as I write.

I went to boarding school at Rosinka's insistence. She paid for it, of course. St Dolores in Jeolikote took me in. It was smarter, more posh than my mother's Alma Mater, St Anne's, but they didn't teach me much. I was in the fifth grade when my mother married again. My stepfather was a widower, an army officer posted in Bangalore. I saw less and less of my mother after that.

I had a stepbrother I didn't know much about. But a stepsister? Who *was* Nina, and what was she talking about? There was a mystery here, a muddled, messy mystery my instincts warned me to steer clear of.

Nina was sitting in the kitchen, staring at a book before her, as if unsure of what she should do with it. Iti noticed the dark roots of her blonde hair, her chewed-up nails, her vulnerability. She struggled to collect herself against the onslaught of memories that Nina's assertion of being related to her had sparked off. Her memories of this house, her claim to it and to Khata Khumani, belonged to her alone. Not to this imposter.

She fiddled with her phone out of habit. No signal. No social media. No messages. No updates. No alerts.

'None of that here,' Nina said smugly. 'No signal. No outside world. We live in a cocoon—or by a lagoon! Would you like a fried egg? Some coffee? Let me get it for you, please.'

As she set about measuring coffee and cracking eggs over a pan, Iti noticed Nina's practised hands—opening cabinets, finding the right switches, knowing exactly where she must reach to get what she needed. Unlike Iti, there was no lapse of memory. It was as if Nina really did belong to The Dacha.

The coffee was strong and fragrant. Nina had disappeared after placing the French Press and the double fried eggs before her. Iti continued to sit in the kitchen, listening to the rain.

The rain in the mountains felt different, sounded different. The insistent tattoo on the tin roof seemed to be conveying some urgent message. Iti was lost in reverie as she listened to its rhythmic beat.

A poem she had read and memorised many years ago surfaced in her mind.

I was not sorrowful, but only tired
Of everything I ever desired.

All day till evening I watched the rain
Beat wearily upon the window pane.

She struggled to remember the rest of the poem. Who had written it? She reached for her phone again, to check, but of course there was no signal.

Ernest Dowson. The name surfaced from memory, like a fish leaping from a pond. That was the name of the poet.

I spent the rest of the day with Badi Amma and Rosinka, listening to their whimsical conversation, their sharp wit, their interrupted stories. Rosinka would take off on some obscure thread of the past, and Badi Amma would break in with a non sequitur. The conversation would meander on after the interruption, or take a new turn altogether.

'And what about you?' Rosinka asked, after their to and fro had run its course. 'What are you up to in the big bad world below? What brings you here, back to never never land?'

I evaded the question, but she persisted. Rosinka was ever the master of persistence. 'Out with it!' she said, tickling me under the chin with her long painted nails. 'Come on, tell us what brings you here.'

'Too much screen time,' I replied reluctantly. 'And loneliness. I needed to hear the rain...'

As if on cue, a streak of lightning lit up the room, followed by a clap of thunder that made the window panes rattle.

The sky grew dark. The lights went off, and although it was only mid-afternoon, the room became shadowy and gloomy. I felt strangely secure, sitting with these weathered old women, so different from each other, and yet so alike. The affection between them was real and tangible, as was their affection for me. I basked in their unspoken love, and drew my chair closer to be able to be heard above the thunderous, clattering downpour.

'I will make some tea for us,' Badi Amma said, reaching out for her cane.

'No you won't,' I said. 'Let me make some masala chai for you, with cardamoms. Or we could ask that Nina...Where is she? And who is she?'

They ignored my question.

'You will not be able to make tea in the dark, Iti,' Badi Amma said. 'I, on the other hand, know my way around blindfolded.'

She got up from her chair and made her way carefully towards the kitchen.

Rosinka turned to me. 'That Nina!' she said, in a voice that could have meant anything.

'Who is Nina?' I asked again. 'Is she related to me? She says she is my cousin...'

'That Nina!' Rosinka said again. 'That Nina can say anything.' Then she fell silent.

Badi Amma returned with the tea in cracked, mismatched cups.

'Why haven't you served the tea properly, Lily?' Rosinka demanded imperiously. The camaraderie between them had dissolved—Rosinka was once again the mistress and Lily the house help.

Badi Amma mumbled something about it being too dark. Rosinka ignored her and began talking about the tea gardens her grandfather had once owned near Berinag. She spoke in English, which was her language for me, as it had been for my mother. To Badi Amma she speaks in Hindi and pidgin Pahari, with a smattering of English words and phrases. After nearly a lifetime working with Rosinka, and some decades living in The Dacha, Badi Amma understands English well enough, but does not speak it. Although she called me 'my darling child' just the other day, when I told her that I missed her the most when I was away.

The electricity returned and the lamp flickered to light again.

'Who is Nina, Badi Amma?' I persisted. There was a mumbled reply I could make no sense of, and which Rosinka's authoritative voice quite drowned out when she launched, all of a sudden, on the story of her Russian grandfather's meeting with Tagore in Ramgarh, after which he decided never to go back and married the daughter of a Scot who had gone native in these mountains.

'Imagine, child. Had he not stayed on, where would we all be?' she said to me. 'And where would *you* be, eh?'

That night, in my room, another line from Dowson's poem rose to the surface of memory before I drifted off to sleep.

I was not sorrowful, I could not weep,
And all my memories were put to sleep.

5. THE DAWN CHORUS

Iti woke up around dawn. An unmusical chorus of birds was heralding the morning. She peered cautiously out of the window. It wasn't yet morning light, but the sky had cleared, a reprieve from the monsoons after the storm of the previous day.

She struggled with the latch and stepped out into the balcony. There was a sound, a movement in the garden. Who could it be? She went back to the room and brought out her phone. She flashed it in the direction of the sound. It was a wet, bedraggled figure, a slim person with blonde hair, tiptoeing through the garden in the direction of the house.

She switched off the phone light. Nina—for it could be nobody but her—disappeared. She had not noticed the weak beam of the phone, travelling tremulously in the half-dark, which had been directed at her back.

Iti could only sleep fitfully after that. When she awoke, golden sunlight was streaming into the room. She stumbled blearily into the kitchen, searching for coffee.

Nina was sitting by the kitchen table. 'Good morning,' she said composedly, flashing a smile at Iti. 'I hope you slept well.'

That afternoon, Iti wrote in her journal:

Nina was sitting in the kitchen again. We didn't talk about her disappearance, or her stealthy return. I smiled back at her, made myself some coffee, and retreated to the sitting room—the 'drawing room', as it has always been called.

The coffee had a heavenly fragrance. It smelt of roses and vanilla and cinnamon. The French Press was an elegant brass frame with a vintage finish. The sunlight, the coffee, the morning air—these things made me smile, until I suddenly realised that something in the image of Nina's composed smile was rankling me.

I went back to the kitchen but she was not there. She had disappeared again.

It didn't rain all day. The clouds crept in mid-afternoon, to form a frame for the skyscape and the valley view. Iti had been off the Internet and digital media for two—or was it three—days now. She kept her phone batteries charged. It was strange to realise that the world below was going on without her. The world below had, of course, always got along without her, she had only lurked in the borders of the frame, but it felt strange to lose even that slender connection.

She sat in the garden, thinking of nothing. Motes of dust danced in the clear sunlight. A magpie swooped down, then retreated. Its harsh chatter broke the quiet of the afternoon as it settled on a low branch of the silver oak that edged the garden.

Rosinka had told her once, when she was a child, that a solitary magpie brought bad luck. 'One for sorrow, two for mirth, three for a funeral, four for a birth.'

'My Scottish grandmother used to tell me that,' she had declared, shaking a finger at the young Iti as she spoke.

The memory flooded into the sunlit afternoon. As if on cue, the two women wobbled into the garden. The gardener had set up a cane table and four chairs near the verandah, and Rosinka and Badi Amma settled there like visiting deities.

They were magnificent. The light in their eyes had not dimmed. Rosinka's eyes were gimlet-sharp, piercing, and Badi Amma's, though calmer, took in everything with the unblinking tenacity of a sophisticated surveillance system.

Nina appeared, carefully balancing a tray in her hands. Four mugs and a pot of tea. Biscuits on a China plate. A bowl of namkin brimming with peanuts and twisty orange swirls.

Iti noted that Badi Amma spooned in two heaped helpings of sugar in her tea, while Rosinka took none.

Rosinka's hands were thin, venous, shrivelled, and yet expressive and full of vitality. Her nail polish was a vibrant violet colour. Badi Amma's hands were freckled and puffy, with the moonga ring biting into her skin.

'Can I pour you some?' Nina said, turning to Iti. The same clean-as-a-slate expression, the cool smile. And brown eyes today. They suited her.

An amused, triumphant smile began to play on Iti's lips. She quickly suppressed it, but Nina had seen it.

'I wore dual-colour lenses yesterday—blue and green. The sky and the grass in my eyes. Today is my earth day.' she explained. 'Maybe I will write a poem about it. How you see the world and how the world sees you—it's all about the lens, isn't it?'

'How many colours of contact lenses do you possess, Nina?' Iti asked bemusedly.

'Only three,' Nina replied. 'Blue, green and brown. I would like a grey pair though, to match the monsoon skies.'

'And what colour are your eyes really?' Iti persisted.

'Black,' she confessed. 'Boring black eyes. One has to work on these things. It's the digital age. We can become who we want to be.'

'Do you have a prescription?' Iti asked. 'Just playing around with these things can hurt your eyes.'

'I go back to my natural black tomorrow.' Nina looked wistfully at Iti. 'I did this to impress you...to get your attention. I had thought perhaps we could be friends.'

Iti was both surprised and shamed into silence.

'Sometimes I think I occupy negative space,' Nina sighed. 'I'm a cipher, a nobody.'

'It's lonely to be alone,' she continued plaintively. 'I want to belong—to people, to a place. You wouldn't understand.'

'I do understand,' Iti said gently. 'I have walked that road all my life,' she wanted to say, but didn't.

She pictured herself with green eyes. It was a good thought.

The magpie began again on its harsh chatter. An army of clouds marched in and took over the sky. It began raining. They rushed towards the verandah. Nina gently led the old women in.

Iti could hear the rain beating staccato on the tin roof of the verandah. The furious downpour continued for about ten minutes, then eased as abruptly as it began. The sky cleared, and a glorious rainbow spread out before them, spanning the valley.

Iti felt a sense of complete contentment, an emotion she was not familiar with. It was as though there was a cellular realignment within her, an emotional homeostasis. Or was it hemostasis?

She felt cradled between the two eternal women and their unconditional acceptance. They were both so different from each other, and yet, in her mind and in her heart, they were one unit, one entity.

6. A LITANY OF LOST LOVES

I had, a long time ago, begun a novel, a thinly veiled account of past heartbreaks interspersed with wishful fantasies. One more non-starter in my history of failed fiction—in the eminent company of *Promises to Myself* and that other work of potential genius, *HypeReality*. I'd called this one *A Litany of Lost Loves*. The alliteration was embarrassing, but something compelled me to go with it. These were three case studies on my love life, written in an analytical mode.

The book was soon abandoned, indeed aborted, but those past heartbreaks continued to haunt me. I was somewhere a romantic, and the idea of the animals walking in two by two into the Ark had made a deep impression on my young mind. And so, at fourteen, I fell in love. His name was Manoj Chakrabarty, the only man in St Dolorosa, not counting the ancient guard at the gate. Manoj had been the art teacher at my school, but he had been fired for unspecified reasons. The girls shared wild speculations on the reasons for his disgrace. Some of the teachers figured in the stories, and there was talk of abortions.

Then he returned to the school, and was mysteriously reinstated to his previous post. One afternoon, while correcting a sketch I had made of a vase of chrysanthemums, Manoj Sir took hold of my wrist and caressed my palm. This sent a delicious shiver down my spine. 'Come to the garden after class and I will show you how to draw a rose,' he whispered in my ear.

I went, dutifully, expectantly. I carried my sketch pad and pencils with me. The rose garden was an abandoned patch of scrub with some unkempt rose bushes which occasionally and unexpectedly burst into flower. They looked drooping and remorseful to my eyes.

Manoj Sir materialised before me. 'There are some beautiful roses behind the trees,' he whispered. 'Follow me.' He wore green corduroy trousers that sagged around the knees. He had long hair (for those times) that touched the shoulders of his brown (also corduroy) jacket. I followed him.

No one could see us now. He attacked me ferociously and pinned me to the ground. Then he pulled off my bloomers and began pummelling at my private parts. 'There is a rose garden there,' he said. 'Your private rose garden. And I can make it bloom.'

I could feel his sharp fingernails digging into my skin. I had frozen up, but a panic button screamed inside me. I kicked him, pulled up my bloomers, and fled.

That night, I tried to reach the secret rose garden. He had scratched me with his long nails. Something trembled inside me, like a wild wind wailing in a valley. I liked the thought of it. I got my notebook and wrote out the words: 'A wild wind wailing through the valley.' It sounded like the first line of a poem. Someday, I would complete it.

The encounter had terrified me, but somewhere, I felt special in being thus sought out. Perhaps this was what happened between men and women. I thought of his battered corduroy trousers, and his long hair that reached to his shoulders. I was shaken, and upset, but not angry.

The next day I went to retrieve my sketch book and pencils from where I had abandoned them, amidst the trees behind the rose garden. They were not scattered about as I may have expected but stacked neatly at the base of a spreading tree. Someone had placed a pink rosebud over them.

It could only be him. I saw this as a romantic act, a sign of repentance and contrition. Perhaps he had been overcome by passion.

Manoj Sir avoided me for the next few days. I encountered him at the corner of the corridor and he bent down to tousle my hair, then quickly moved on. I was confused by my own reactions. I did not throw the rose away, it lay in the corner of the shelf that held my schoolbooks.

Then Manoj Sir went away. We were told that he was on long leave, but he never returned, not at least during my time at school.

Years later—I can't remember exactly when, only that I was living in Delhi—I came across a newspaper report about an art-teacher's death. 'Death by suicide?' the headline read. It went on to describe the strange circumstances surrounding the death of Manoj Chakrabarty. He had been fired from his job in a public school in South Delhi. His body had been found lying on the floor in the school corridor, surrounded by rose petals. The cause of death was poisoning by ingesting paint-thinner. He had also slit his wrists. He had wanted badly to die, though the news report said there was no suicide note. 'The victim's blood had turned the colour of chocolate,' it said. My stomach heaved and I began vomiting. I continued to throw up for days afterwards. I went to a doctor who did some tests and prescribed some innocuous medicine, but that didn't help.

The haze of panic and anxiety that surrounded me after I read the report slowly subsided. I stopped eating chocolate. I went for long walks. I took sleeping pills at night. In a dream I heard myself say: 'I should have let you love me.' I did not see him in the dream, I only heard a low, animal keening.

There was a line of poetry by William Blake that I encountered somewhere:

O Rose thou art sick
The invisible worm
That flies in the night
In the howling storm:

Has found out thy bed
Of crimson joy:

And his dark secret love
Does thy life destroy.

The poem gave me strange solace. The lines became imprinted in my memory, like a signature tune. They took on new shape and meaning, and in some sense absolved me.

And in any case, I told myself, the individual sickness we are born with will always take us in the end. Who can really save anyone?

I don't think of Manoj Sir any more, and wonder how and from where he wandered into this journal today.

═══

The other lovers—there is one whose name I have forgotten. I sit up at night sometimes trying to remember it.

Peter?

Michael?

Johann?

What was it? How could I possibly forget?

He was Danish. We met in Goa. We got along. He smelt of soap. He was nice, and uncomplicated. He made me smile. Sometimes, we laughed together.

He returned to Amsterdam. I got a message once, saying he was planning another holiday in India, and would I be around. I replied that I would, and then he fell off the map. No further communication. I lost his phone number. I forgot his name. Perhaps he forgot mine.

'Iti…' he had asked. 'Short and sweet! What does it mean?'

I struggled to reply. I was never sure about my name and what it really meant.

'It means the end of something. Like a full stop. It can also mean a new beginning,' I responded lamely.

'That's nice!' he said. 'It's really sweet.' He gave me a kiss on my cheek. Perhaps he had already decided it would be an ending. Not a new beginning.

I woke up with a start last night after writing this. I had suddenly remembered his name. It flashed in my forehead like neon lights on a lonely billboard in a dark road. His name was Matthew.

With the passing years I recused myself from hope and gave up on the coupledom dream. I register average on the looks front, though I suspect it's getting better with age as I have been consistent in size and shape and continue to look much the same as I always did. I'm not exceptionally charming or well groomed. The pool of available men is receding like a village pond in a drought year. I am not yet inclined to turn to my own sex for comfort.

It's my dream to meet a man who is kind, considerate and successful, a man who loves to read and remembers anniversaries and birthdays. A man like the one on Raymond suiting advertisements, the complete man.

Not so long ago, I fell in love with someone who looked like the complete man. He loved music, and I accompanied him to a piano concert, and to a Thumri festival. I did my best to look soulful and immersed in the music, and when he reached out to hold my hand, I responded with just the right amount of warmth and reciprocal pressure.

We were compatible, I suppose. He took care while rolling on his condom and rolling off his socks (in that order). The earth didn't move. I didn't like the smell of his aftershave. I lay in his arms but they didn't feel welcoming.

X (I remember his name but choose not to record it) was a chartered accountant. After we had been dating for a while, he sat down beside me. 'I feel I've got to know you, Iti...' he said, '...and to trust you. I want to ask you something.'

Was he leading up to something?

'You know that I'm a chartered accountant,' he said, 'but that's not what I'm like inside. I'm wildly imaginative.'

'Accountants can be very imaginative too,' I murmured.

He looked suspiciously at me to see if I was being facetious. 'I'm very creative, in my inner self. And I'm writing a novel. I've been writing it for years. Well... you are an editor. I wanted to show it to you. It's a very personal, very private narrative. I've shown it to almost nobody...just a few friends.'

He coughed, and looked down at his socks. They were red with white polka dots.

'Will you read my novel please and tell me what you think? Perhaps you could even edit it? I would pay you, of course.'

'I will read it as a friend,' I replied. 'Of course I will. And of course I wouldn't accept any fees.'

'Should I email it to you?' he asked anxiously.

'I'd prefer a hard copy,' I replied. 'In double space, please.'

The novel. That was the beginning of the end.

For some reason, X had printed it out in a cursive font. In a way, that was a reprieve, as the sheer awfulness of the writing took more time to register.

If I have been true to anything in life, it is to words. I don't compromise with clarity and stylistic integrity. I believe in words, and narratives. I know even as I write this that it sounds grandiose and ridiculous. But it is also true. So I'll let it stay.

There are more important things in life than books, I'll be the first to admit it, but words are sacred. I sometimes think that at the root of all the tragedies of this world are words used without care, without understanding.

But I was talking about a failed love affair. About X. His novel was titled *FOR WHOM THE BELL TOLLS*. Seriously, and no exaggerations, not even the all caps. It was dedicated to 'The Master—Ernest Miller Hemingway'.

I tried to read it but couldn't get very far. It was written in the first person. The narrator wore red socks, when he wore socks at all. There were guns, and a turbulent sea, and a green-eyed girl-woman with breasts like cantaloupes. There were a lot of exclamation marks.

I was fascinated, and repulsed. It was clear from the way he wrote—from the adjectives, the references, the jokes, the situations he put them in—that X didn't like women. In fact, he despised them. There was a well of resentment deep within the gentlemanly exterior.

Some element of self-preservation surfaced from within me. I stepped back, indeed, I ran out, from his life. I didn't answer phone calls, or emails. Nothing.

My stony silence must have surprised him, especially as he was eager to interact with the editor-on-the-cheap, the editor-in-thrall, that he thought I was. His phone calls and messages became more frequent and more frantic. I began enjoying his panic. I found myself returning to his manuscript to sneer at it. I would plumb new depths of self-obsession, machismo and narcissism with each re-reading. Perhaps it was destined to be a best-seller, I reflected—with other red-pill alphas, if they read books.

There were several memorable quotes. 'Faint heart never fucked fair lady'—a line X had snitched from the internet. Another gem: 'There is nothing a woman despises more than a faithful Beta.' I read this wrong the first time. I thought X was writing about a beta, a faithful Indian son. Until I realised the line was about adored Alpha men and unsuccessful Beta men.

The novel—if it could be called that—could have been compelling in its sheer ugliness, had it not been also repetitive and boring.

A week into my strictly imposed silence, I received an enormous bouquet of red roses from X. There was an accompanying card. 'I guess you must be immersed in reading FWTBT. Giving you all the time and space in the world. I know what editors are like.' A smiley emoji accompanied this thoughtful message.

At first the FWTBT acronym confused me. 'One lives and learns,' I told myself. And then the bulb lit. FWTBT. For Whom The Bell Tolls.

That was the moment of my most lasting epiphany. I didn't need roses. I didn't need a man in my life. I didn't need a FWB (Friend with benefits, in case you are wondering). I was all right alone and on my own. Or so I told myself.

My epiphany was not about a feminist sorority or a gynocentric universe. It was just the realisation that I was ok with myself and I didn't need a man to make me complete. It's a giant step for every woman when she takes it.

Another week passed before I wrote out a longish response to him via email.

Dear X,

I read your manuscript. As an editor, I felt FWHTBT lacked clarity, cohesion or purpose.

As a reader, and someone who knows you socially, I was alarmed by the level of misogyny it displayed.

I suggest you show it to some other editor for inputs.

Regards,
Iti

Radio silence. I got a missed call from him a few days later, which I ignored. Then an email which simply said, 'Thanks a lot'.

The book was published, by a vanity press, under a different title. X sent me a signed copy. There was an inscription: 'To my first reader and critic'.

7. INHERITANCE—I

I keep my phone fully charged at all times, which was never the case in the big city. Of course, there's no connectivity on the hill. I decided to put it to good use by recording Rosinka's memories.

'All right!' she said. 'All right!! Let's take a trip into the past—but light me up first. I need a cigarette.'

She extracted a cigarette and a silver filigree lighter from a pouch that lay beside her and held it out in her claw-like hand.

I looked at her aghast. 'You are too ancient to smoke!' I exclaimed.

'Come on, come on, dear child!' she wheedled. 'I will just hold it, like a fire-stick. I won't inhale—I'm too old to inhale.'

I obliged her. The cigarette smoke, the smell of rain, the wafting scent of dhatura—it added to the magic of the moment. She shut her eyes and pretended to inhale. Her eyelids were powdered over with mauve eyeshadow. I waited.

Her eyes remained closed. Had she nodded off to sleep? Ash was dripping from the cigarette in her outstretched hand.

She suddenly woke up and sat upright. 'My story…' she said dreamily. 'I'll tell you my story. You will have to believe it.'

She took a long drag on her cigarette—a real one this time—and blew a perfect smoke ring in my direction. Then she dropped the cigarette on the wooden floor and stamped on it with a foot encased in a faded red moccasin.

The smoke ring had dissolved, but for a brief second it had framed my vision of her. I will never forget this sight, I thought.

'My grandfather was a Russian folklorist,' she began. 'Some people thought he was a spy, but no, he was a scholar and an explorer. An adventurer. Those were the days of the Brothers Grimm, and of the revival of the fairy tale. Like Wilhelmina and Jacob Grimm, my grandfather Ivan Lobov was also an academic and a philologist. He was my Nana. I never met him. I have the book he wrote up in my room.'

'You said you had a Scottish grandmother…' I intervened. 'Was she his wife?'

She began coughing—a sharp, rasping cough. I grew alarmed and went to the kitchen to get her some water. When I returned, she had dematerialised. I could hear her clumping up the stairs, and followed her—but she had already gone into her bedroom. 'Let me be,' she said from behind the closed door. 'The past doesn't exist. I don't want to visit it.'

I decided to let her be for the next few days. It would require patience to record her memories. But I was in no hurry.

I tried to recall the key facts about her life, but they were sketchy in the extreme. I trawled through possible clues that might be cached around the house, but that didn't yield much.

Rosinka and Badi Amma were having their afternoon nap. The house was quiet. I crept around, trying to decipher the memories and their residues that lived on in these silent rooms.

The room towards the back of the house was once called 'the library'. There were no books there now, just a heap of mouldy cartons and spooky looking piles of something covered up in dusty sheets.

The walls were alive with paintings. They were beautiful, familiar and begrimed. I could see mountains, and clouds, and fungal patches.

I had once edited a book by an amateur art historian. She had spoken of cleaning up an old painting with slices of bread. That's what I did.

The first one was a Roerich. A Nicholas Roerich. The second one bore his signature as well. The third was unsigned. They were all undated.

I was full of my discovery, but did not share my excitement with anyone. I would tread cautiously.

We were having dinner. The gardener's wife, Parvati, had prepared a magnificent pahari meal of yams and carrots and a potato and pea curry.

'Where is Nina?' Rosinka asked. There was an edge to her voice.

Badi Amma shook her head noncommittally, in a movement that could have meant anything. 'Where is Nina?' she asked Parvati.

Parvati replied with an expressive shrug.

'But who is Nina?' I said, in a voice a fraction louder than I had intended it to be. They both ignored my question and continued to eat the potato curry. Parvati had retreated back into the kitchen.

After dinner, Badi Amma asked Parvati for some masala tea.

'Would you like to have a glass of excellent wine, Iti?' Rosinka demanded. I declined her offer.

'Get me some brandy, Lily…' Rosinka said to my grandmother.

'I'll get it,' I said, though I could see Badi Amma shaking her head as though indicating I should not.

The bar cabinet had a key dangling from it. Inside was a well-stocked bar, with whiskey and vodka and gin, and a row of empty bottles on the bottom shelf.

'The Remy Martín,' Rosinka commanded, 'in the green bottle.'

I did as I was told, and returned to the dining table with the bottle and two snifters.

'I will join you, Rosinka,' I said. Badi Amma observed us watchfully. 'Let's sit near the fireplace,' she said.

'So who is Nina?' I asked again, as we sat before the dying fire. 'She says she is related to me.'

'Nina says she is whoever she thinks she is,' Rosinka said, '... at that moment, that is.'

I was getting impatient with their games.

'What are you trying to hide, you two?' I asked, trying to keep my voice calm. The cognac burnt my throat, but soothed me as it made its way down.

'Nina is not related to you,' Rosinka said thoughtfully. 'If at all she is related to us, it is to me, through a long and circuitous route. But she doesn't know that—and there is no need for her to know that.'

'But how—and when—did she get here and establish herself as your adoptive granddaughter?'

Rosinka continued to sip her cognac. 'Granddaughter?' she said. 'It's interesting that you should say that. Every relationship cannot be so easily categorised. She belongs here, too, in her way, just as you do.'

It wasn't a snub or a put down, but the subtext was clear—at least to me. I decided to switch tack.

Rosinka was on her second round of cognac now.

She smiled as she swished the amber fluid around in her mouth.

'I discovered the most beautiful paintings in the old library,' I said. 'Two original Roerichs.'

'Ah yes,' she replied. 'And there is a third one too, but it is unsigned.'

'They are so compelling,' I said enthusiastically. 'Compelling' is not an easy word to use in everyday conversation, but I did. They *were* compelling. I didn't tell her I had cleaned them up with bread from the kitchen.

'What's compelling?' a voice enquired cheerfully. It was Nina, in a demure buttoned-up flannel nightdress, with her hair in two braids. The eyes were black.

'The Roerich paintings in the library,' Rosinka replied. 'The two of them. And there's a portrait of me that Elizabeth Brunner painted, a lifetime ago.'

'They are worth a fortune,' she continued, tapping her long painted nails on the table. 'That's why I don't tell anybody about them.'

Badi Amma asserted herself. 'Time for everyone to sleep,' she said, picking up the bottle of cognac. 'I hope you have had your dinner, Nina, because you won't get any now.'

'Don't worry—I'll fix something for myself in the kitchen,' Nina said. 'Goodnight Grandma Rosinka! Goodnight Grandma Lily!'

She didn't mention me. 'Goodnight little Nina!' I said sweetly as we made our way to our bedrooms.

I awoke the next morning to an urgent pecking on the windowpane. It was the magpie—the one I had begun thinking of as 'my' magpie. It was trying to set up communication, I thought. I stepped out into the balcony. The bird flared its plumage and flew away.

It was a day of patchy sunshine and intermittent rain. I decided to go for a walk and set off in the general direction of Khata Khumani, where my grandmother's old house was situated. The landscape was no longer as pristine as it had once been. Endlessly mushrooming construction confronted me.

As I turned the nape of the hill, my phone came suddenly alive. I was connected to the world again. There were messages from publishing companies, two anxious authors, a tirade from someone I didn't know, and a slew of messages from my school WhatsApp group. I would respond to them later, I told myself. Sometime. All of that seemed far away, somewhat unreal.

Some serious construction was underway to my right. A line of mountain mules carrying building materials slung across their backs waited patiently to unload their burdens. 'The Elysian Condominium—A Mountain Paradise' was coming up.

I retraced my steps to return to The Dacha. It was disturbing to see how quickly the world was encroaching on it.

I sat in the garden for a while with my magpie for company. It chattered urgently in corvid dialect before circling overhead and then abruptly flying away. It dropped something bright and glistening on the ground as it glided past.

It was a ring. A golden ring set with an irregularly cut garnet. An old ring. I thought I had seen it somewhere, but I couldn't remember. I took it inside with me. I could imagine it on Rosinka's clawed hands, with a matching shade of nail polish. It must surely be hers, picked up by the thieving magpie and now returned.

The two ladies were in cheerful spirits. Nina seemed to have made one of her periodic disappearances. I measured out the coffee and waited for it to brew.

They were talking about the past. 'Do you remember when...'

Friendship. How fortunate they were, to have each other, I thought wistfully.

The warmth of Badi Amma's and Rosinka's relationship. The ease of it. It makes me look at my own life. Friendship can be a good substitute for love. You need courage for both, I think, and I never had that—the courage to risk affection. And you need faith—in yourself, most of all. I've never had that, either.

I'm in the mood to blame something for this. Blame someone. In Badi Amma's face I see my mother's. I see her in mine too, sometimes, when I can bear to hold the image. It is her I will blame. It is that kind of night.

What was it about me and my mother? When I am with Badi Amma I feel enhanced, enabled. I feel connected, part of her, and she becomes a part of me, even though we are not remotely like each other. Rosinka stimulates me, she brings me alive, although I remain critical of her, and indeed wary. And she loves me—she does.

But my mother. If she was my mother. She depleted me. Was she afraid of me, or of the part of her life that I represented? She approached me with the defeated air of a habitual loser, or of someone who had never even tried.

What was the damage?

She ate into my entrails. She was empty, she was hollow. She was not equipped to face life, and that is the disease she gave me.

She was incompetent at living, a failure at facing life. That at least was my construct, and possibly an unfair one. But then, I never knew her. I had to imagine her, conjure her up.

She had survived my father's abandonment and found another life, another family. She had carried on, leaving me behind. She had been brave in her way, and ruthless.

No. I think she was just flotsam on the blind river of life. A rag doll. She did not choose anything, she went where the current took her because she had no will of her own, not a thought in her head.

I struggled to love my mother. I did. But it ended in disaster, always. I remember the time I made a new year resolution to reach out to her. I tiptoed into her room and put my arm around her. We had been reading

Little Women at school, and something in the story had sparked my resolve to be a loving daughter. I kissed her awkwardly on her cheek. Her armpits stank. Her woollen sweater had a tired, musty odour, which was layered with the smell of garlic and onions from her joyless labours in the kitchen. And there was another smell, I couldn't pinpoint it, but it was malodorous and revolting.

I gagged. 'Ugh!' I exclaimed, and pushed her away. My mother's face crumpled. She looked as if she would cry, but she held back the tears.

I felt repentant, and reached out to stroke her arm, as though she were a friend's puppy I was being kind to. Then I disengaged myself and left the room. That was the last time I ever reached out to her.

8. INHERITANCE—II

And so the days passed, in the habitual timelessness that was a part of life in The Dacha.

One afternoon, Iti set about snooping gently around the house, searching clues and giveaways to Rosinka's past for her archiving 'project'.

When she went into the old library room, a shock awaited her. The two Roerich paintings were not there. They had disappeared from their frames.

Someone had inexpertly and hastily cut them out. Jagged corners of paint and canvas clung to the gilt frames. To Iti it felt as though she had stumbled on the scene of a murder. It was a violation, a sacrilege, a desecration.

What was I to do? It would not help to go screaming to announce the theft to Rosinka and Badi Amma. They were not ready for shocks at their age. I would wait for them to wake up from their siesta and tell them when they came out for tea.

I went off in search of the Mali, Pooran da, and his wife Parvati. Somebody had to be told. The thieves—I thought of them as a duo—might still be prowling around the house. There were so many strangers—tourists and taxi drivers and construction workers and real estate agents—milling across Kumaon.

Then sudden panic set in. Were Badi Amma and Rosinka safe? And Nina?

Parvati was sitting in the back garden, staring at the vegetable patch. 'Come with me, Parvati!' I said, and dragged her in with me towards the house.

First Rosinka's room, with its heavy hanging drapes. She woke up at my first knock. 'Come in, Iti,' she said composedly. 'What is it? You look in a panic.'

'I wanted to talk, Rosinka,' I blabbered. 'There's been a theft—in this house—here!'

That seemed to amuse her. 'The big thief is prowling around every day,' she responded. 'But we two ladies are not letting him in. No Sir!!' This was followed by a little laugh, a giggle, really.

Then to Badi Amma's more modest bedroom. There was a framed photograph of my mother as a schoolgirl, and one of Neem Karoli Baba. I felt oddly bereft that there was no photograph of me there on her wall, or on the bedside table.

Badi Amma was snoring gently. There was a bubble of spit by the side of her mouth. Parvati and I tiptoed out of her room. She would wake up soon.

Downstairs again, to Nina's room. We knocked but there was no response. The curtains were drawn and it was dark inside. I switched on the light and Parvati drew the curtains to reveal a pretty view of the back garden and the vegetable patch, with pumpkin flowers on a creeper.

She wasn't there. Some dirty clothes lay scrunched up in a corner. The bed was a mess. The unmistakeable smell of weed hung over the room. There was an unused sanitary pad lying on the floor.

The room looked as though it had been hastily abandoned. A sheet of lined yellow paper on the table carried a message.

'To Badi Amma and Rosinka. You Abbandonned me. Everybody Abbandonned me. Except Avinash. He is a Painter and Artist. I am going away with Him. I am taking the Expensive paintings as my dowry. They are also my inheritance after all. Yours, Nina.'

Later, I shared the note with Rosinka. I thought she looked relieved. 'Well, that's that,' she said. 'Maybe she will find a happier life somewhere. But I don't like the name Avinash. It sounds somehow ill-omened.'

I had expected Badi Amma to be more concerned, but she was impassive. Her face was a mask and she said nothing.

'But they were expensive paintings!' I exclaimed. 'They were priceless. You should call the police!'

Rosinka smiled indulgently. 'They were only paintings, dear!' she declared indulgently. 'Splodges of paint on mouldy canvas. There's more to life than that.'

'Nina has slashed them,' I said. 'You must do something.'

'Youth is wasted on the young,' Rosinka said ruminatively. 'I was young too, once. There is a desperation to being young.'

A mischievous glint entered her eyes. 'Were you ever young, Iti?' she said speculatively. 'I think perhaps not.'

I took that as an insult, a personal jibe. It hurt. I tried to ignore the barb, and to turn it around. 'You, Rosinka, on the other hand, are evergreen—forever young,' I replied gallantly.

Badi Amma entered the conversation. 'The paintings matter,' she said, 'but so does Nina. She is young and foolish. We must find her.'

'Find her we must,' I said. 'Perhaps we should alert the police. But what I want to know—what I *need* to know—is if I'm related to Nina.'

Badi Amma took my hand in hers and stroked it gently. She looked me in the eyes.

'No, Iti, Nina is not related to you—or to me, or to your mother. For the rest—it's best that you ask Rosinka.'

Rosinka was signalling with her eyebrows to Badi Amma. 'Don't say anything,' she whispered.

'I can hear you, Rosinka, I'm not deaf yet,' I said sharply. 'Please clear this stupid mystery.'

'Nina is allegedly my husband's sister's grand-daughter,' Rosinka said grandly. 'That sister lived in this house for many years. Your grandmother knew her. A silly woman. Even a bit retarded, perhaps. How I despised her.

'This sister—my sister-in-law—she had a daughter who ran away from home. Her boyfriend left her pregnant, and then she left the baby in an orphanage before doing the decent thing and dying. That child was Nina, whom the family brought back at some stage.'

Rosinka was always frugal with facts. That was a lot of information for her to give away. There was more.

'That side of the family had filed a case in court claiming a share in this bungalow. I had to use pull and push and pay through my nose to settle it. Then this Nina comes here, claiming a share in this property. I don't know who set her up to it—most of that lot are dead and gone. I'm much too old to take that sort of nonsense, so I told her that she was Lily's grand-daughter. And your blessed Badi Amma played along. After all, *her* peace of mind was at stake as well.'

'You lied to your grand-niece?' I asked.

'Of course I did,' Rosinka replied off-handedly. 'Can we close this conversation now? It really is none of your business, Iti.'

The Dacha didn't seem so idyllic anymore. Two ancient crones using their authority and power to mislead a young girl. It was the sort of thing that would come naturally to Rosinka, but for my grandmother to play along—no. Not nice. Not nice at all.

I walked away from them, and to take my mind off their duplicity, I went back to the library. I wasn't looking for clues, now that I knew Nina was the thief. I went because the third painting, the one that hadn't been taken, still intrigued me. I pondered the mystery of this unsigned painting. A pahari woman, standing in a field of flowers, draped in a mustard and vermilion Kumaoni pichauda. She wore a traditional large nose ring, a nath, and a heavy silver necklace. She had no face.

The style was deliberately naive with a touch of ironical modernity. Who could the painter be?

And looking at the empty frames beside that strange painting, I was reminded of Nina. In a way, without a face herself. What did she know of herself? What *could* she know?

That evening, I could feel Nina's absence sharply. It was tangible, like a reproach. Where was she now? What was the colour of her eyes today? Who was Avinash?

The young are vulnerable, and sometimes stupid. They hurt easily. I was worried about Nina.

She was lost, that much was clear to me now. And she hadn't a fraction of the strength of the two women with whom she had sought shelter, perhaps, as I had.

The two women, Rosinka and Lily—so different in their lives and trajectories, but here at this vast age they had become merged to almost a single presence, a co-dependent entity. Today, after what Rosinka told me, with Badi Amma listening, I was faintly repelled by their self-absorption, by Rosinka's indifference to Nina's fate, but I was also drawn to their immersion in life, and their determination to live it on their own terms.

I will record Rosinka's life, and Badi Amma's too. There is nobody to do it but me—no one to chronicle and remember. Their stories too will be slashed out of their frames like the Roerich paintings were.

I have persuaded Rosinka to tell me her story. She can draw it from memory or weave it from fantasy as she wishes. Some of Badi Amma's stories will surely emerge from hers. And when Badi Amma shares her remembrances, Rosinka will certainly figure conspicuously in them. How could she not?

Badi Amma and Rosinka. One of them, Lily, wise, stubborn, and accepting of her years. The other, 'The Countess on the Hill', vain and full of vitality, continuing to dream and desire. Which of them represents the life force? Perhaps both. In their entwined ways.

9. THE CAFÉ AND THE CAVE

The journal had become Iti's constant companion and confessional. It was a beautiful lined notebook she had bought at a bespoke stationary boutique in an expensive mall. She had a special blue-ink gel pen that she felt suited the mood and style of her notebook. Her words were flowing fast and furiously. But her sprawling handwriting and the double space she habitually used meant that the pages were running out. This caused her a nagging anxiety. She decided to go in search of a new notebook.

Parvati told her of a café a few kilometres down, at

the intersection of the highway, which stocked books and notebooks and suchlike. 'And expensive coffee and stale food,' she continued. 'You might also meet some old friends there.'

It was a pleasant walk down, despite the signs of construction all along the path. The café was charming, with Internet and books and organic millet cookies. It had a board that announced rooms on rent. Iti ordered a masala chai and looked around her. There was a stack of postcards on display. They were pretty but faintly eerie mountainscapes in a butter paper folder. 'Instagram Poet and Artist Influencer Avinash travels with you through the Himalaya', the folder said in silver print.

That was the name of Nina's boyfriend, whom she had run away with. But not very far, it seemed.

'Can I see your rooms please?' Iti asked the young man with Rastafarian locks who sat at the counter.

'All our rooms are full up,' he said, 'but there's The Cave if you are interested.'

'The cave?' she asked. 'That's an interesting name. Never heard of anything like that before.'

He gave her a friendly wink. 'You've never seen anything like that before, either,' he said. 'The most unique holiday experience anywhere. I can show it to you if you like. It's just a short distance away.'

She looked at him, surprised that she found him almost likeable, although she was almost certain he had been Nina's accomplice in the theft of the Roerich paintings.

'So do you want to see it? The cave?'

Iti nodded.

I nodded. I had to track Nina, and any leads were welcome. He led me out and pointed to a motorcycle parked by the side. 'Your steed, my lady,' he said, winking again. We set off. He had left the café unattended.

The cave was just that—a cave. There was a wooden bench and a small fenced garden in front of it. A screen door and red gingham curtains led to a neat space with looming rock walls. It had a bed, a washbasin, and a battery-powered tube light.

I gasped. It looked terrifying. I felt claustrophobic. 'Not for me,' I whispered, and stumbled out.

'There's an outdoor bath and loo,' he continued. 'Tourists love it.'

'Who—what conceived this?' I asked. 'And why?'

'Real estate,' he said, winking again (Perhaps it was

his substitute for a smile). 'My uncle used to meditate here. I took it over when he passed on.'

We returned to the café. I bought a lined notebook. 'I'm Iti,' I said. 'Iti Arya.'

'I know,' he said. 'And I'm Avinash.' He didn't wink this time.

I decided to let this play out, to give nothing away. It was best to discuss it with Rosinka and Badi Amma first.

'Great to have met, Avinash!' I said. 'I will be in touch.'

I saw someone peering cautiously out of an upstairs window as I left. It could have been Nina. It could have been anyone.

I brought up the matter with Rosinka and Badi Amma, but they seemed to already be aware of Nina's whereabouts.

'We are old people,' Badi Amma said. 'We don't need trouble. We don't want trouble.'

'That girl appeared out of nowhere,' Rosinka said. 'And now she has disappeared into nowhere. She was trouble and that's why I took pains never to provoke her. Let sleeping dogs lie.'

'But she has not disappeared into nowhere,' I said sharply. 'She's just down the hill with her boyfriend. Do you know what those paintings were worth? She could creep in any time to steal and plunder. She could kill the both of you—*murder* you!! And me!'

'She would be doing us a favour,' Rosinka declared. 'We have made a suicide pact, your grandmother and I. When we feel that the burden of life gets too heavy, when either or both of us fall ill, we shall withdraw from life. I have the suicide note ready, signed by both of us. And my revolver.'

She said it without irony, without humour. My heart lurched. 'But Badi Amma doesn't know how to shoot. She has never handled a gun!' I said wildly, clutching at straws.

'Your grandmother is an excellent shot,' Rosinka replied calmly. 'We are not immortals, Iti. We cannot live forever. We have to plan.'

Badi Amma nodded her head in agreement and gave me a smile.

'What about this house?' I asked. 'What will happen to it?'

'We will talk about that another day. We are alive as of now, and we plan to stay alive for a long, long time. You had asked me about my past—about the old days. I thought we could spend the evening going through photographs. I have kept them ready. A sort of "Show and Tell".'

She nodded to Parvati, who had been listening in. As if on cue, she brought out a large ivory-coloured metal trunk and placed it before us. It had a sheet of white paper tacked on with scotch tape. 'Rosie' was scrawled across it with a purple marker.

'Rosie?' I asked.

'That is Nina's name for me,' Rosinka replied. 'Affectionate, I presume. She helped me sort these photographs out.'

I noted that she said 'is', not 'was'. She had not let Nina out of her life yet.

We started going through the photographs. They were in various stages of disintegration. The older albums were better preserved. There was Rosinka sitting in a restaurant, her hair piled up high, multi-layered danglers hanging from her ears. An eager-looking man with a cauliflower nose was gazing at her adoringly.

'Paris...' she said. 'A long, long time ago. That's my husband. He was no looker, as you can see. That's why I decided never to have his children. And the other options never worked out.'

'Don't you need spectacles, Rosinka?' I asked

curiously. 'I can't see beyond my nose without them.'

'Eyesight reverses again with age,' she replied. 'It's called "second sight". I could thread a needle for you if you wanted.'

She turned another page of the album in her lap. 'Look at this one…me at the Gateway of India. We were staying at the Taj—the old Taj—in the most wonderful suite.'

And so the photographs progressed. She looked scintillating and sparkling in all of them. Dark lipstick (a deep, rich black in the still glossy black-and-white print), eyeliner, immaculately arched eyebrows, hair in a chignon or hanging loose. The jewellery looked expensive and authentic.

'Where is all this jewellery kept?' I asked.

'It's safe,' she said offhandedly. 'I'll show it to you some day.'

I thought of the ripped Roerich canvases. 'The hills are no longer as safe as they were, Rosinka. You and Badi Amma need to take care now. There are all kinds of strangers around', I cautioned.

'I'm going to have some haldi and milk,' Badi Amma said placidly.

'And I will have a hot chocolate with a drop—a

peg—of brandy in it,' Rosinka declared. 'Lily, do ring the bell for that Parvati. She must have scuttled off to her room again.'

'All these photographs are indoors,' I observed, 'except for the garden parties and picnics. And yet you chose to live here, in The Dacha, amidst the great outdoors, all your life.'

She looked at me wisely. 'I lived here, I live here. I belong here,' she said. 'This is my life. The photographs—they are just memories.'

She began singing, in a wavery, quivering, but well-modulated voice.

Should auld acquaintance be forgot…
and nevverrr brought to mind?
Should auld acquaintance be forgot
And the days of auld lang syne?'

Badi Amma had joined in too, singing an eccentric mix of English and Pahari, but the rhythm and lilt perfectly matched to Rosinka's. Everything about the moment, the pathos, the courage, the camaraderie, will remain etched in my heart.

Rosinka handed me the album. 'This can go back. If I

were really vain, I would ask you to pull out photographs from the bottom of the trunk, most of them from my verrry green years!' she laughed.

'We must see them now!' I said and dived in and brought up a stack. A large black-and-white photograph slipped out. It was a portrait which had been touched up with colour accents. I recognised the face.

'I'm bored of this,' Rosinka said suddenly. 'Put all this away. Some other time.'

I had never seen her young, of course, but I knew instantly it was her. She was wearing an enormous nose ring which covered much of her face. A traditional Pahadi pichauda was draped around her shoulders. There was something else about the photograph that was familiar—it was framed in almost exactly the same way as the third canvas in the library. Though that portrait displayed no facial features, it was surely modelled on this one.

'Badi Amma?' I whispered, turning to her in wonder.

'Yes, it's Lily,' Rosinka said acerbically. 'The photograph was taken by my husband. He was more than a little fond of your grandmother. Wasn't he, Lily?'

A subdued smile broke across Badi Amma's wizened face. 'Yes,' she said simply.

'And the painting? The unsigned painting?' I asked.

Rosinka's mood had turned sour. 'Paintings paintings paintings!' she snapped. 'Can't you talk of anything else? That's enough for today, I've told you. Let's pack up the trunk and disperse.'

She had a last slurp of the brandy and hot chocolate, leaving a dark red lipstick imprint on the porcelain cup. Then she was up and moving towards the stairs, thumping her walker on the floor.

Badi Amma didn't follow her. She stepped out into the verandah, then began walking around the garden.

I followed her out and gave her a hug. 'I love you, Badi Amma,' I said. She stroked my hair and smiled. Her eyes were glistening with tears in the moonlight.

10. ROSINKA'S DREAM DIARIES

Arthritic fingers and pens that leak ink are not the only way to write. One can write on water, or even thin air. The elements are always receptive, if sometimes volatile.

I do not know when I woke up from my dream of last night. I could hear the owls—To Whit Too Whoo—and then the sound of a train chugging up the hills. We have no trains in these hills, we never did, so that midnight express to never-never land was dredged up from my dreaming imagination.

The Kalka-Simla toy train line was set up in 1903

to connect the new Summer Capital of British India with the dusty sweltering plains. I wasn't yet born in 1903, although my mother's womb had held her other children, my brother Alexis, my brother Nicolas, my sister Galina.

In my dream, I could hear the owls, and the train, and then I was in it, in the shadowy compartment, holding his hand. The hills unfolded before us, visions of pine and oak and deodar, with floating cloud banks and sometimes a solitary wispy presence.

He was holding my hand, stroking it absent-mindedly as he read a newspaper spread out before him. Then we entered a tunnel and everything went dark, and he sought out my face, caressed me, and began kissing my lips, searching deeper and deeper.

And then we came out of the tunnel and he stopped kissing me and began reading his newspaper again. This happened again, the dark tunnel, the touch of his lips, his hands, the gold band on his ring finger.

There were three owlets inside the train, and their eyes glowed and glittered in the dark as they studied us when we kissed each other in that dark tunnel.

In dreams, as in life, it is difficult to keep track of the passage of time. I do not know how many tunnels we passed or how many times he kissed me. When I woke up, I wanted only to return to that dream, so I shut my eyes tightly and willed myself back to that train and the dark tunnels and the joy of being kissed.

These days I wake up with a start. My mouth is often dry, and I am no longer sure which of my limbs are attached to my body. It seems impossible to be up and about, and there is no real reason to be. So I drift back to sleep, will myself back to sleep. I try to hang on to whatever fragment of whatever dream I was inhabiting, clutching at it like Ariadne's thread to lead me back to the labyrinth.

When I awoke today I wanted to urinate, but I was too tired to get up. I had been dreaming of a fragment of red velvet which was somehow floating before my eyes. I was wearing a mask, the sort one would wear for a masquerade. A wisp of hair floated before my left eye. I was already focusing with difficulty because of the elaborate golden mask. As I insinuated myself back into this dreamscape, a blonde woman came and stood before me, arms akimbo. She was wearing a red velvet cape. Her smile turned into a snarl. Her teeth were golden and glinted in the candle light. A waiter appeared, holding a tray and a bottle of wine. She poured the wine over me. It smelt sour. 'Acetic acid and acetaldehyde,' I remarked, not at all perturbed. I was drenched and the sour smell of the wine woke me up.

I had urinated on my bed.

I struggled to get up and made my way to the bathroom. There is a pile of pretty hand towels with cross-stitch embroidery I keep by the sink. I soaked one in the freezing tap water and doused it with cologne. I sponged myself carefully before I stepped out and knocked loudly on Lily's door with my cane.

Lily was awake, of course she was. She came to open the door. There was a maala in her hands and she was still counting the beads and mouthing her prayers to some imaginary god.

I told her what had happened. She followed me into my room and examined the damage. I felt shamed, and humiliated, but we are both very old. It could have happened to her.

I would never have cleaned up after her but she did so ungrudgingly. She removed the sheet and under-sheet and left them to soak in a bucket in my bathroom.

'Why don't you take this bucket to your bathroom, Lily?' I said. She took the bottle of Dettol from the medicine cupboard and poured some into the bucket. Then she lumbered out wordlessly, carrying the bucket with her.

She returned soon enough, and laid out a large pink bath towel on the bed.

'You can lie down again,' she said. 'The quilt isn't wet. I will get you some tea.'

I was grateful to her. She didn't say 'you haven't wetted the quilt'. She said 'the quilt isn't wet'. I appreciated that.

I haven't noted any dates on these dream diaries. It makes no sense, as dreams exist outside of time. The past, the present and the future float by each other wordlessly. As do our days. Will death be another dream or will it be the awakening from a dream? I suspect it will be darkness, and closure.

I am terrified of death. It shows up in my dreams as an invisible, unwelcome visitor. There is a train waiting for me in a deserted railway station. It is night time and there is no one on the platform except a disembodied presence that informs me that my baggage has been loaded. The train is like a serpent waiting to strike, it is as empty as the platform, the lit-up compartments show no human presences.

The train does not leave. I return home to rest, although my luggage is loaded.

This dream recurs again and again. It leaves me full of dread. I find myself wishing that it was daytime, and longing for the hustle and bustle of a normal Indian station, with children and chaiwallahs, porters and pickpockets.

After the death dreams, I wake up with a dull head and a pounding heart. I wish I could light up a cigarette as I sit on the pot, but I've given that up.

My familiar silk kimono. My pills for the day, though sometimes I decide not to take them. Then coffee, and sometimes news on the radio. The day dawns.

It's like riding a hangover. But Lily makes a good cup of coffee. She is sulking today, I wonder why.

Maybe I will take the sleeping pills again, the ones the doctor prescribed.

The most lurid and horrific dream of them all.

I am lying on the kitchen floor, weeping. Lily appears carrying a pot of hot water. She is holding it with kitchen gloves, *my* kitchen gloves. She pours the water over me and I am in hell. I am writhing and screaming. Like a savage pahari, she has boiled nettles—shishuna—in the water. She puts her gloved hands into the steel pot and takes out a bunch of wilted nettles. She rubs these over me, on my arms, on my feet. She scrubs my face with the nettles.

I wake up. My arms, my legs, my face, are burning. I am on fire.

Of course this has happened, in reality, in time, outside of this nightmare. A lifetime ago, I did this to her. Now she is haunting me, possessing me, taking her revenge.

I am giving up on these dream diaries. They don't exorcise anything. Best to forget one's dreams, obliterate one's nightmares. I will take the sleeping pills regularly now.

I might even take an overdose. It might be the best way to go.

I might even leave a suicide note, blaming it all on her.

11. BADI AMMA'S MEMORIES

'My mother's home-village was like paradise. We had three lemon trees which yielded the most enormous golden fruit. We had a plum tree, its fruit sweet and juicy—"pulumb", we used to call them. And a kaphal tree. We were a prosperous family—my maama, my mother's only brother, was the village mukhiya, the Sarpanch. My father had died, so my mother had returned to her nanihaal to bring up her two daughters. There were three of us and we grew up in a household full of cousins and other children.'

Badi Amma's voice was gentle, wistful. I was

recording her memories on my phone. She was much more cooperative and compliant than Rosinka.

'I dream of those days every night,' she said. 'Then I got married to your grandfather. His village was right next to ours, but I travelled a long distance, from a prosperous home to a poor one. My maama had his own daughters to marry off, and there were the three of us, so I had no complaints. And your grandfather was a good man, he had some fields and a house his father had left him when he became a sadhu. His wife—my mother-in-law—followed the husband in his wanderings some years later. Your grandfather was fourteen or fifteen then.'

'He had no brothers or sisters?' I asked.

'No. I think *we* were like brother and sister, because we only had each other! He was a good man. But he left the world too early. I was nineteen. It was TB that took him. Pahari men used to die early in those days. All their bad habits—and the life was rough too. We women were stronger, we were tougher. Although we used to smoke beedis too and were fond of tobacco, I won't deny that.'

'Lilleee…!' we heard Rosinka calling. 'I better see what she wants,' my grandmother said, and lumbered out. She stroked my hair and my forehead as she left. Her hands were rough, work-worn, as they had always been, yet incredibly gentle in their touch.

I wasn't in the mood for Rosinka's sharp comments, so I didn't follow Badi Amma. I spent my time loping around the house, looking for windows into the past. I went back to the library to examine the unsigned painting. Who was it by? Could it be Roerich? Did he know Rosinka and her husband? Where was the portrait by Elizabeth Brunner?

I crept into Nina's room. There was no need to be surreptitious, but it still felt like the scene of a crime somehow. Parvati had tidied it up and made the bed. She had left the sanitary napkin on the small desk, though the dirty clothes had been removed.

There was a notebook I hadn't noticed before. It was captioned 'Nina—The Poems of an Impossible Romantic.' Impossible was spelt 'Immpossible'. The editor in me was too pained to examine it further.

I went back to Badi Amma's room, and when she returned, we began where we had left off.

'I was working for Rosinka when your grandfather died. There was no reason not to, she paid a good salary and treated me well, and we needed the money. She changed my name from Leela to Lily and I didn't mind that—in fact, I quite liked it. She was so beautiful in those days that I would just stare at her in adoration.

It was as though she had descended from Indralok or something.

'Rosinka had only to enter a room for it to be bathed in fragrance. There was a perfume—I remember that it was called Joy. It was her favourite. I loved that perfume! Once I even stole a small vial of it—though she would have given it to me if I had asked. And then of course I never dared to use it. She would have discovered that I had stolen it. I hid it away and smelt it sometimes, to make myself happy.

'My sister, my elder sister Kamla, came to live with me. She was widowed too. She could read and write a little—the missionaries had taught her. She used to look after your mother when I came to work.

'Kamla was a wonderful cook. Her paptaula! Her dubke, her bhatt ki chudkani...there was magic in her hands. I told her to come and work here with Rosinka and Peter Saheb, but she flatly refused. She was much too proud.

'Now Peter Saheb—he loved pahari food. Sometimes I would get Kamla to cook something specially for them. He loved her shikar bhaat, her meat curry and rice. She would marinate the meat overnight and then slow cook it for at least three hours. Then she would smoke it with a little lump of coal for less than a minute.

'Rosinka hated pahari food—she called it junglee. She had trained cooks from Nainital and Bareilly who made lamb chops and cutlets and stew and things like that. And now we two old women have to make do with Parvati's cooking! The less said about that the better.'

'I will cook something for you,' I offered gallantly. 'A mutton curry like Kamla used to make. I will look up the recipe for that shikar bhaat on the internet.' Then I remembered there was no internet, that I had done without it for weeks and not even noticed.

Badi Amma smiled and continued. 'Peter Saheb. His full name was Peter Paul Singh. He was half angrez—his mother was from Germany. His father's family were sardars. He didn't wear a turban but he wore a kadaa. He had a big heart. He and I were friends. He could speak a little Pahari and used to talk to me in our language. Sometimes, he made me sing Pahari songs for him.

'Peter Saheb was writing a book. He was translating the book Rosinka's grandfather had written in Russian, which had also been translated in German. He was writing this in English—from German—but he wanted me to explain the stories to him. So he would test these stories on me in Hindi and broken Pahari and ask me if they sounded all right, or if the Russian and German writers had got confused.

'I will tell you those stories sometime. I must have told you some when you were little. They were so funny—and so true! We would laugh and joke as we told each other stories. "You are my researcher," he would say. "My native informant." That's what he would call me—his native informant.

'Now Rosinka did not like it. Not that I was doing anything wrong. I was working hard and doing all the tasks and chores I had to do. But Rosinka did not like it—not one bit.

'Peter saheb had broken his nose in a boxing accident when he was young. I thought he was very good-looking in spite of his nose. But not Rosinka. "We are beauty and the beast," she used to say. Or she would call him "Cauliflower"—phoolgobi!

'Peter saheb never minded these insults. He would take it all as a joke. He adored her, we all did.

'One day something very bad happened. It was the day before Holi—it is a day I can never forget. Even now, when I hear the songs of Holi echoing across the hills in the month of Chaitra, I put cotton wool in my ears and lock myself in my room.'

'What happened?' I asked apprehensively. I could feel the dread and the pain that was overtaking her.

'They had a fight,' Badi Amma whispered. Her head was bent down and her voice heavy with memory. 'Rosinka had been drinking all day. Glass after glass of wine. I could hear her screaming at him. They had been squabbling all week, but today was different. Kamla had cooked some shikar bhaat for Peter saheb. She had come with your mother—she was still a little girl—to deliver it. We were in the kitchen when Rosinka came raging in. She took the food from Kamla's hands and threw it on the floor.

'Then she slapped me. Once, twice, thrice, four, five times. Then Kamla stepped in. She couldn't bear to see her sister insulted. We were self-respecting people. She pinned Rosinka to the floor and dragged her by her hair across the kitchen. She rubbed her face in the food that had fallen on the floor. There was rice and meat curry all over Rosinka's face and clothes.

'Rosinka was too shaken to attack back. She sat cowering before Kamla. Your mother hid behind me, sobbing. She has never forgotten that day, never forgiven me for it.

'"You have committed many sins today," Kamla said, in a voice as cold as a mountain glacier. "You have insulted anna—the food I brought you. You have insulted my sister, who is faithful and loyal to you. You have frightened my niece, who is but a child. You are a piece of turd."

'Saying that, she led me out of the house. Peter Saheb appeared and understood what had happened. Rosinka was sitting weeping on a chair now. There was food all over the upholstery. He slapped her. "I didn't do anything," she sobbed. "They attacked me for nothing."

'There were red welts over my face which spoke for themselves and told him the truth of the matter. But I kept my dignity. I didn't snivel or grovel.

'"There is one more sin you committed," I said to Rosinka. "That animal lost its life for nothing. It died in vain."

'I realised even as we walked out that what I had said was somehow irrelevant. We had all calmed down by the time we reached our home in Khata Khumani. The cows mooed their welcome. I hugged them and held them close. Then we had the rest of the shikar bhaat, the portion Kamla had saved for home. The lamb had not died in vain.'

Badi Amma was gasping as she told the story. I held her tight and tried to soothe her. I reached into the pocket of my quilted jacket for a handkerchief. The uncut garnet ring that the magpie had dropped in the garden fell out, right there, into her lap. She clutched it and held it to her heart.

'Where did you find this?!' she asked in between her sobs. 'I was looking for it everywhere. Peter Saheb gave it to me, when I came back.'

'Please go away now, Iti!' she pleaded. 'Let us not return to the past. It was all a long time ago. I have forgotten the past. We have each other. We have this house. We have you. We have our remaining days.'

I didn't know what to say, how to respond. 'I will never bring up the past again, Badi Amma,' I promised. 'Let's sit in the verandah and have some tea together—all of us.'

The tumultuous succession of memories had shaken me up. I went to my room, and listened to the recording on my phone. Then I went to the balcony and lit myself a cigarette from the emergency stock in my medicine pack.

I rarely smoke, but sometimes it is the only thing to do.

There had been a break in the monsoons and we

had had some sunny spells, but the curtain of cloud over the northern ranges had kept the snow peaks from view. As I sat there that day, the clouds cleared, and I could see the snows. There was Nanda Devi, the sacred peak of Kumaon, silent, inaccessible and enigmatic. The two sisters, Nanda and Sunanda, were the guardian spirits of Kumaon. Nanda Devi spoke to me now, through the mists that wreathed her, counselling patience and kindness.

I didn't feel up to encountering Rosinka and Badi Amma, they would probably be sitting in the verandah fronting the house having their afternoon tea. I slipped out through the kitchen entrance and walked along the hedge to stay out of sight. I intended to walk to the Café to check my internet, and also find an authentic recipe for shikar bhaat. There were some lamb chops and frozen cuts of meat in the fridge.

There was of course another motive. I wanted to meet Avinash and find out more about Nina's mysterious non-disappearance.

I enjoyed the walk down. When I got to the Café, I found Nina in the pebbled front garden. She wore enormous sunglasses and a bandana and was pouting at her camera. She didn't notice me.

There was nobody at the café. No guests, nobody at the till. I waited for Nina to notice me, but she didn't. I found a recipe for Kumaon mutton curry and saved it for reference. I checked my messages. The school WhatsApp group was busy with their usual cheery chatter. I replied to my professional emails. I caught up on news of the outside world. Forest fires in Borneo. Forest fires in California. Sea levels rising. Glaciers melting. I skipped the political news. I read up the new film releases, viewed their trailers. I waited for Nina to appear.

It was Avinash who appeared, and greeted me warmly. 'Where's Nina?' I asked. 'I wanted to speak with her.'

He looked evasive. 'Who's Nina?' he asked. 'I have a sister named Nina but she lives in Mumbai. Works in advertising.'

'I must be confused,' I replied. He was texting somebody, possibly warning Nina that I was there. I ordered a coffee and drank it to the dregs. I read through some old newspapers. Then I left.

It had begun to drizzle as I set off for The Dacha. It was a steep walk uphill and I was soaked by the time I returned. I went to the spare bedroom downstairs to towel myself dry. I would borrow a hair dryer from Rosinka—she must surely have one. Or several.

This was the room Nina had stayed in. I looked for the notebook with her poems. 'Nina—The Poems of an Immpossible Romantic.' But there was no notebook there. It had disappeared.

Rosinka offered me her hair dryer. My grandmother offered to help me dry my hair. It continued to pour. The sound of the rain beating on the tin roof drummed into our heads. The lights flickered off. We sat in darkness until I lit some candles.

'Can I have some brandy please, Rosinka?' I asked. 'I think I'm coming down with a cold'.

Badi Amma led me to the bar and opened a new bottle of cognac. 'I will have some too,' she said. 'I think I need it, today.'

'Me too!' Rosinka said coyly. 'Three for company!!'

We drank quite a bit that night. There was something about the dark and the flickering candles that encouraged us. Nobody got drunk. We were all alert, in our different ways, to deceptions, to betrayals, to mortality.

'Come and sit here next to me, Iti,' Rosinka said. I did as commanded. She smelt of an elusive floral fragrance. Was it Joy?

Rosinka read my mind. 'It is a secret formula. I sometimes smell roses in it. Sometimes magnolia. Dead, burnt leaves. Nettle. Yes, nettles too, I think. A lot of things.'

Then she said, 'You may as well know. I have made a will. You inherit everything. Not that silly Nina or her relatives. It's a watertight will. No complications. Let's raise a toast to that.'

I was shocked. Bewildered. Confused. I remained silent. Rosinka pinched me in the dark. 'Say something, girl!' she exclaimed.

I said all that was expected—expressed my gratitude, kissed her wrinkled face, wept. But inside me, I was still processing this strange turn of events.

'And if I die before her, which I probably shall, you must look after Lily. I know you will. That double suicide plan—it isn't practical. I realise that.'

I was coming down with a cold. I couldn't make sense of anything anymore. I gave her another kiss. I hugged my grandmother. 'Goodnight, ladies,' I said. 'I'm overwhelmed. I'm also coming down with a cold, and I don't want to pass it on to you. I'm going to sleep. Love you and leave you.'

I negotiated my way up in the dark with the aid of a torch that Pooran had provided. We had not eaten anything. I heard Rosinka asking Parvati to rustle up some parathas and red chilli achar. 'The immortals,' I muttered to myself. They were truly both destined for immortality.

I passed out as I hit the bed. I awoke feeling dreadful. My head, my nasal cavities, my throat, were all in revolt. I was worried that I might have passed on the bug to the ladies when I kissed them goodnight, and resolved to remain in quarantine until I was better.

This house. The Dacha. Rosinka had willed it to me. It was to be mine. It would be mine. I couldn't believe it.

The cold got worse. I developed a fever. There was no reprieve from the rain. It poured without a break for three days. There was no electricity—the generator didn't have the capacity to cope. No water, as the pump couldn't power the water up.

Parvati and her husband saw us through heroically. They would rush about, sometimes outdoors, sometimes indoors, in raincoats and gum boots. There had been a cloud burst, and there were landslides and floods everywhere.

We were comparatively safer as we were near the top of the hill, and so not rained down with rocks and boulders. The garden was devastated, and the road leading to The Dacha had given way.

I ventured down for meals, but tried to keep out of their way. Pooran would tell us grim tales of cars being crushed in landslides, and houses collapsing into chasms and rivers. I signalled to him to stop, thinking it might upset the ladies, but they told him to go on. They seemed to relish these tales of devastation, and nodded their heads sagely at each new disaster.

We did not speak of the will, or my inheritance. It seemed unreal, and I let it remain so, like a conversation in a dream.

I lay in bed huddled under the quilt, trying to shut out the sounds of thunder and rain. Badi Amma came into my room. She did not generally venture upstairs, and I reproached her for straining herself.

'I had to talk to you,' she said. 'Half-truths are never the whole truth. Rosinka has been good to you, she is gifting you her house and all that she has. My house too, the house in Khata Khumani, will come to you. Not to your mother, who will sell it and spit on the money.'

That made logical sense, but it shook me. I was engulfed by a sense of compounding responsibility. I thought of my rented room in Gurgaon, of the smells and sounds that I inhabited there. Perhaps it was time to return from this dream, for dreams have the potential to become nightmares.

'The roof of the house in Khata Khumani has collapsed. The old house is rained out, though the wood is intact. Some of the slate tiles flew off the roof and landed in a neighbouring house. The neighbour was trying to tether his cow, which had run away. They both died, the man as well as his cow. It was lightning, not the tiles.'

It was a grim tale. I shuddered. There was another clap of thunder outside, followed by lightning. I thought I heard a scream.

'But that's not what I came to tell you. I told you only half the story the other day. Half-truths are never the whole truth. Let me tell you how it ended.

'I promised myself I would never return to that house again. Kamla made me take an oath too. A week later, Rosinka came to Khata Khumani to beg my forgiveness. "I didn't mean it," she wept. "I was possessed by an evil spirit. Please forgive me, Lily. You are more to me than my sister."

'That infuriated Kamla. "I am her sister," she said. "This is our house. I would like to explain this to you—she will not come back, even if God himself came to persuade her. We mountain women don't care about your riches. We give our loyalty where we get respect. And we are polite to our guests. Would you like some tea?"

'Rosinka appealed to me again. I could see that she meant what she said. We were friends, after all. Then she left.

'Two days later, I found Peter Saheb at the door. Kamla had taken the cows to graze in the bugyal. Your mother had gone to school. We were alone in the house.

He looked at me. He held my hand. He begged my forgiveness.

'"You are my friend," he said. "I cannot bear to see you insulted. Rosinka is selfish and stupid. She is jealous of you. But she too loves you, in her way."

'I was shocked. "Why would she be jealous of me?" I asked. "Rosinka madam has everything. I am her servant. Her humble maid."

'"She is jealous because she does not understand friendship," he said. "Or loyalty. Rosinka is hard and shining outside but she is lost and hollow inside. You must understand that."

'"Peter Saheb," I said, "you are my friend. If you tell me to return, I will."

'Of course Kamla was upset with me, and your mother too. But I had to return. This was my home. It is still my home. And yours.'

We sat together in silence for a long time. The

shadows darkened even further. I lit a fragrant pillar candle that Rosinka had sent up via Pooran. Was it Magnolia? Or Lily of the Valley? I could not tell.

'One more thing,' Badi Amma said. 'After what happened with Rosinka, I had changed. I had to settle some scores. I had never thought of Peter saheb in that way—even though my husband was dead. I was a widow, I was alone, but I kept my distance.

'We were friends again, as we had been before. But something had changed. I had changed. I allowed love to flower between us. We were like a man and a woman together. Once. And then twice. Then I said to him, "Peter saheb, I cannot live in this house like a namak haraam. I eat your salt, Rosinka's salt. We will be like a brother and sister from now."

'Peter Saheb understood. "Yes, Lily," he said. "I understand and it shall be as you say."

'That's when he gave me the ring, the ring you found again for me. He called Rosinka and gave me the ring in front of her. "I have sardar blood in me, Rosinka," he said. "Lily is my sister. I am giving her this ring as a gift. Please respect my sentiments and honour them."

'He died the next year. But we were friends, and also lovers. I want you to understand that.'

It was still raining outside. I felt a wave of futility, of sorrow. She was so brave, my Badi Amma. She was trying to teach me something, tell me something. I would treasure the secret she had shared, that she had trusted me with.

Perhaps it was not too late. Perhaps I too would find love. Someday.

'What happened to your sister?' I asked. She remained silent for a while.

'A terrible thing happened to Kamla,' she replied at last. 'She had taken the cows to pasture. There in the beautiful meadow above the hill, in that calm and quiet bugyal, her fate was awaiting her. There were still tigers in these parts in those days. A tiger that had injured its foot, a man-eater, had been on the prowl in the next village. She must have been sitting peacefully, watching the clouds, taking in the scent of the flowers, when it attacked her. The baagh tore her to pieces and dragged her away. The villagers went in search of her. I went with them. We found the silver hansuli she had been wearing around her neck. A trail of blood led to her body. What remained of it.

'We Pahari women have a hard life…' she said, 'but we are strong. Strong as the mountains. As you are, Iti. You must never doubt that.'

And she left. I thought about her life, and the story she had told me. I thought of the thieving magpie that returned her ring to me. I thought of the photograph Peter Saheb had taken of her. And I thought of the painting, the unsigned painting that Nina had left behind. Who had painted that? I dreamt of the painting that night, and then the faceless face melted into the image of my school friend Anita Shivdasani, she who had killed herself when she was twenty-five. What did it mean? What was I to learn from that? Probably nothing.

Badi Amma came to see me again the next morning. I was beginning to feel better. My grandmother brought me a cup of strong ginger tea and some lightly salted namakpaaras. The tea tasted like nectar, and the namakpaaras gave me sustenance.

'It's too early in the morning to talk about these things,' Badi Amma said, '...but when I told you all those stories from the past, about Rosinka and her savage ways, I felt lighter for having shared those hurts, those unbearable humiliations. Sometimes it is self-destructive to allow people to cross the line—in love, or in hatred. I allowed Peter Saheb to cross these lines, in letting our love flower. I allowed Rosinka to cross these lines, in all that I have let her do to me. Perhaps it was my guilt that led me to forgive, or at least to forget the things that she did.'

My head was still heavy and I was a bit alarmed by the vehemence in her voice. But I could see that she had to speak to me, to give voice to all that lay buried so deep in her heart. She was like a river in spate.

'I was brewing some nettles this morning, to make a nettle soup. I thought it would help you recover. My grandmother used to make it for us grandchildren for this season. So I plucked some leaves of shishuna—of nettles—and put them to boil. There was a tall patch of nettles by the corner of the kitchen wall. I plucked them and put them in the brass pot I sometimes use.'

'It sounds like witchcraft,' I said. 'Chudail Vidya. And how did you pluck the nettles? I sense that you are an accomplished witch, Badi Amma, but did you use plastic gloves?'

She smiled. 'We call it "daayan ki chai" here in the hills,' she said. 'Rosinka has a name for it, an English name, but I forget, some difficult word…'

'Witches' brew?' I said.

'Yes, yes. That is what she calls it. But you were asking how I pluck them. Now, there is a trick to nettles. You hold them hard, with all your strength, and they do not hurt. But if you are cautious, and afraid—if they brush against you, graze against your skin—then nettles hurt and sting and burn.'

I was awake and alert and listening to her carefully. What was she trying to tell me?

'It's like the truth, Iti. Confront it, hold it firmly, no evasions, and you can handle it. The truth has to be held fearlessly, like a stinging nettle.'

'So where is the famous nettle soup?' I asked, trying to sound bright and cheery. 'Though I'm glad you got me the delicious ginger tea instead of the daayan ki chai. Maybe we can have the witches' brew for dinner instead.'

But she wasn't listening to me. Badi Amma was mumbling to herself. She seemed to be floating in her own world.

'What Rosinka did to me,' she said. 'I had forgotten it—I had willed myself to forget it. But it is like a wound that has healed, but acts up in some weather.'

My grandmother. I stroked her arm, fondled her wizened skin.

'"I can never forget it"—that seems like such a big thing to say,' she continued. 'Too big and also foolish, because we do forget, forgiveness comes in, and the texture of memory changes. I can't even remember all that happened that day. Let me go over it for you, at least what I can remember.'

She waited for me to start recording.

'The nettles reminded me. This was after Peter Saheb had died. There was just her and me in the house—the two of us, alone. We were both grieving and hurting in our separate ways.

'Rosinka came into the kitchen, humming a song and dancing to it. Her face was flushed and there was a demonic smile hovering around her lips. I wondered if she had been drinking.

'She lifted the cover from the pot and inhaled the smell. Nettles smell funny when you cook them—sort of sharp and green.

'"What are you cooking in there?" she asked.

'"I'm boiling some shisuna," I replied. "Nettle soup is good in this weather."

'She came and gave me a hug. Yes, she had been drinking, I could smell it on her. She started giggling. "I know something that's even better for this weather," she said mischievously.

'She made me sit down on the kitchen chair, turning it to face the wall. "I have a surprise for you," she said, planting a kiss on my cheek. Then she covered my face with my black shawl, the one I always wore at home. "Now shut your pretty eyes," she said.

'I did as she said. It was pointless to argue. Besides, I was feeling suddenly very tired, the hurt of Peter Saheb's death had hit me like a slap once again.

'Rosinka put on the radio and some English song began playing. The singer had a sweet voice, she sang like an angel. I could sense that it was a sad love song.

'Now Rosinka came from behind and yanked my shawl off. She held the pot of boiling nettle brew in her hands. Then she threw the boiling water over me. Luckily, I turned my face away just in time. But the water fell on my hair and neck. I was on fire. And the music, the sad song, kept playing on the radio.

'I hid under the kitchen chair. She threw the rest of the boiling water over my legs. Then she took the nettles and began rubbing them on my feet. She had put on cotton kitchen gloves. I gave her a kick and ran out of the kitchen—after all, I was—I am—much stronger than her. I ran towards the outhouse. Before I bolted the door, I plucked a bunch of palak leaves from near the patch of nettles.

'Palak leaves are the antidote to nettles. They grow together, always. It's nature's balance. Perhaps Rosinka and I are like the nettles and the palak leaves, an antidote to each other.

'I took the palak leaves and rubbed them all over my skin. I lay on the floor and wept, in anger, in sorrow, in helplessness. I stayed in the outhouse for two days. Rosinka came and knocked on the door that night, and the next, but I did not respond.

'I did not talk to her for a week after I returned. She was quiet too, and very kind and loving, as though nothing had happened. Nothing at all.'

I listened aghast. Words failed me. 'That is the most savage story I have ever heard,' I whispered. 'We want nothing to do with her. Tell her to tear up her will. Come back with me. We could live in Gurgaon together.'

But I knew even as I spoke that Badi Amma would never leave The Dacha. She belonged here. As I did.

12. THE HEAVENS DESCEND

The young are different. That may be a generalisation but it is also true. I too had known youth. As a teenager, I too had felt the sap rise within me. But my situation and circumstances and the strained dynamics with my mother led me not to freedom or rebellion but rather to caution. Caution bordering on fear. It wasn't only fear of failure, of sorrow, but a fear also of success, of happiness—what price would I have to pay for these things? What would they demand of me, and would I have it in me?

'Were you ever young, Iti?' Rosinka had said. She

could tell. I had never taken a shot at life; I was never young.

And then there is Rosinka, still so miraculously young. Resolutely, joyously young in spirit. But she would have watched out for herself at any age—not for her the vulnerability of youth. Or so I imagined.

Nina, too, is young. But foolishly young, so utterly lacking in either instinct or experience. She is rash, vulnerable and defenceless. Life's learnings await her. Will she learn?

Nina's story took a completely different trajectory during the deluge, in that week of rain and storm.

The rain eased for a day and then the downpour began again. There were floods and power outages with general devastation everywhere. The Dacha was an island in the chaos, where life continued as it had. There was no electricity for long stretches and the generator had given up the ghost, but other than that, we carried on.

The ladies seemed none the worse for wear. Pooran had discovered some old kerosene lamps which he would light in the evenings. We had spare batteries for our torches and a never-ending supply of scented candles from Rosinka's caché. News of the outside world filtered in from the maali's quarters as he had a television set which caught Doordarshan and other channels.

That afternoon Pooran came in looking solemn. 'I think…I fear I have some sad news to convey.' He coughed. 'There is news that Nina—our Nina—is trapped in a landslide. They are searching for her but they are losing hope.'

Rosinka's face went white. Badi Amma remained impassive. I was filled with dread.

'Nina is our kin,' Badi Amma whispered. 'She is Peter Saheb's niece. You must go with Pooran, Iti, and find out what has happened. See how you can be of help.'

Rosinka gave my grandmother a warning look. Then her face recovered some of its colour. 'Yes, Iti. Lily is right,' she said. 'Nina is your cousin. You must see how we can be of help.'

'I will go to the Café to check out the situation,' I said. Pooran accompanied me and we set off down the squelchy path. It was raining steadily. The road was in ruins. I slipped once and fell, but no damage was done except for muddied clothes.

There was a large crowd assembled outside the Café,

braving the rain. A local television crew was interviewing Avinash. 'She will be safe,' he said. 'By the grace of Nanda Devi she will be safe.'

I followed him as he headed to a waiting vehicle. It was an open jeep with a policeman in the driver's seat. 'I'm coming with you,' I said. He nodded, and Pooran and I squeezed in. A convoy of cars and the blare of sirens followed us.

We arrived at the cave. The Gola river flowed beneath us to the right. It was in full spate. I could see collapsed houses and floating debris below me.

An eager camera crew was waiting outside the cave. The pretty bench and the small enclosed garden had disappeared—the landslide had claimed it all. There were rocks and boulders and upturned trees everywhere. A rescue team was at work, chipping steadily at the debris. Nina was trapped somewhere within the cave, where the mountain had reclaimed her within its womb.

The rescue team was manned by sturdy determined dotyals with muscular thighs. They wore yellow helmets and fluorescent jackets and safety harnesses. No shoes, only rubber slippers. They were humming together to keep pace as they hammered away at the avalanche of mud and rock that blocked the entrance to the cave.

Suddenly they stopped singing and stepped back. An enormous snake had slithered out from between the morass. It must have been at least ten feet long. It had the distinct markings of a king cobra. We watched with fear and fascination. The assembled crowd was in shock, but not for long. Mobile phones were whipped out to record the moment. The television crews were having a field day as well. They pushed and jostled until there was a mini stampede.

The rescue team was still, they knew a sudden movement could provoke the serpent. The cobra observed the crowds and proudly raised its crown and hissed. The crowd cheered. Pooran pulled me towards the car.

'That snake is the guardian deity of the cave,' he told me. 'These fools don't know anything. Let us pray for Nina's safety.'

Someone from the camera crew tried to throw a pebble at the serpent, but was restrained by the crowd. It had already retreated by then, and returned to the embrace of the mountain.

I thought of Nina, trapped inside, in the dark damp entrails of the cave. Was she still alive? Why had she ventured there?

The rescue team had made a breakthrough. The boulder they had been cautiously dislodging had yielded a narrow entrance. They got out their torchlights and strapped on safety ropes to each other. The human chain crept in as the crowds outside raised a cheer.

Avinash tried to crawl in too but they restrained him. It had stopped raining. My heart was pounding.

We waited for almost an hour. Two of the men came out and signalled for a stretcher. The small entrance had been bolstered up with a frame. Two more men emerged, pulling at something or somebody. It was Nina.

I tried to inch through the crowd to catch a glimpse of her. Her face was coated with mud and grime. She seemed barely conscious but a faint smile played on her lips.

A makeshift ambulance took her to the Army grounds, from where she was air-lifted to the government hospital in Haldwani. Her ordeal had made her a national heroine. Posts about her with photographs and poems had gone viral. The poems she had posted on social media were finding keen audiences. An article in a major newspaper had a long piece asking 'Who is Nina?'

We returned home. Badi Amma and Rosinka were waiting anxiously in the verandah. 'She's alive,' I told them. 'She will pull through.'

I returned to the café in search of Avinash the next morning, but he was in Haldwani at the hospital. I started scrolling through my phone. The Internet was patchy but I felt compelled to catch up with the world. I still needed it, I still belonged to it.

13. EVERYWOMAN

Days of glorious weather followed the deluge. My magpie sunned itself and dried its plumage. The owls peered out cautiously. They looked happy.

There was a leopard on the prowl. It was a 'kukuriya baagh', the sort that habitually attacks dogs and small animals, but this one seemed emboldened, and more adventurous. It had leapt on a young girl who had been returning home late at night from her job as a receptionist at a guest house. She had survived.

Nature seemed too close for comfort. This was not a romantic idyll—it was a struggle, a battle. And the tourists, the visitors from the plains, were not helping.

Parvati cautioned us to stay indoors after dark. 'No need to stroll out and admire the moon,' she admonished.

But step out I did. It was late at night. The moon was high in the sky, but it seemed very close. I felt that it was smiling at me, speaking to me.

Then I heard a strange sound, familiar but unfamiliar. It was as though someone was sawing at a log of wood—but that couldn't be, so late at night.

Then the smell, an awful putrid stink, wafted to my nostrils. It was the leopard on the prowl.

I didn't scream or run. I tiptoed back to the verandah and then rushed inside. My mountain genes had cautioned me and seen me through.

Rosinka was enthused and excited when I told her about it the next day. 'I wish I had been there,' she said. 'I shot a tiger once, when I was young. We used to go on shikars, then. Those were the days!'

And these were happy, convivial times, too. I would sit with the ladies in the evenings and joke and laugh. The city and my work tried to pull me back, of course. I had fled here on an impulse, but now it was only rational and sensible to return. I couldn't live here forever—or could I? How long would that be—forever?

'Do you think about death, Rosinka?' I had asked her once.

She had cackled wickedly. 'Well, Death thinks about me a lot. Death thinks about me all the time!'

There was talk of a fibre landline coming up that would enable digital connectivity. That would enable me to work remotely. I would be able to watch Netflix. I could reconnect with my school WhatsApp group. I was beginning to miss them, their updates, and their affectionate concerns.

Rosinka was especially excited by the idea of getting an Internet line. She had been trying for a long time but there was a sort of overhang, a connectivity shadow, that had disabled it.

Pooran was sent to investigate the status. He came back with a message from Avinash. He wanted to come over and visit Rosinka and Badi Amma. Rosinka was wary about meeting him, but he turned up the next day anyway. He looked drawn and defeated.

'How is Nina?' I asked. 'Is she back? Is she well?'

'Nina is back,' he replied, '...but she is not well. She has fractured her foot. She's bruised and broken and very shaken up. In short, the dreadful accident has left her a wreck—though she's being very brave about it.'

He hesitated. Then he said, 'I was hoping you would allow her to return here, to The Dacha. To rest and to heal. She needs to be looked after...by women, by family. I've tried, but I'm not what she needs just now.'

'What happened between you?' Rosinka asked. 'Why did she run away to that cave in the middle of the deluge? It sounds cruel to say this, but she brought it upon herself. That girl is trouble. We are old people. I don't think we can handle more trouble.'

Avinash handed Rosinka a cylindrical roll he was carrying with him. 'Here are the Roerich paintings,' he said. 'The ones she stole. I had no part in this. She said she brought them with her as dowry.'

'That's absurd,' I exclaimed. 'A theft is a theft. Does she have no moral compass? And to damage works of art—what sort of person would do that?'

'Nina isn't quite grown up yet,' he replied. 'But she's a good person. She has had a difficult life—and now the most traumatic experience possible. Please give her another chance.'

'She wanted us to get married,' Avinash continued. 'I told her that I wasn't ready, that I needed some more time. That's when she took the keys to The Cave and zipped off on my motorcycle in the middle of the night.'

He sighed again. 'My motorcycle is destroyed too. It's pulverised. And I won't get any insurance, as it was an Act of God. I tell you, I loved that motorcycle.' There were tears in his eyes.

'That girl is trouble,' Rosinka said again. There was an ominous note to her voice. 'But we will take her back. She is family. It is very difficult to tolerate stupidity, but sometimes it becomes necessary.'

All of us heard her, and let her words sink in.

'Can I get you some tea, Avinash?' Badi Amma asked. He nodded gratefully.

'Can I see the paintings?' I asked. 'I hope they have suffered no further damage?'

He unrolled them and laid them out on the dining table. They were magnificent. It was as though they carried the very spirit of the Himalaya within them, of the snow and the sleet, the pines and the firs, the clouds and the sky. I was moved to tears to have them returned here to us, to The Dacha, where they belonged.

'Can I bring Nina back today?' Avinash asked, hope rising in his eyes.

Rosinka nodded her assent. 'Get her,' she said. 'We will take her in.'

Then she swung into action. Parvati's niece, Sunita,

was summoned to be nurse and keeper for Nina. 'We need someone to keep an eye on that girl,' she said. 'Sunita has an MA in Sanskrit. She will be able to manage things. She is probably the same age as Nina.'

I couldn't understand the train of thought there, but Rosinka was right. Sunita took charge the moment Nina entered The Dacha. Avinash brought her up in a taxi. She was in a wheelchair, with her leg in a cast. There were scratches and bruises on her face and arms. Her hair had not been brushed for a long time. She looked grateful to be back, but she wouldn't speak to any of us. Sunita wheeled her to her room.

I stepped out into the garden, taking in the sounds and smells. Cows mooed somewhere in the background. Cars honked, as the new exodus of tourists had begun. Spider webs glistened with diamonds—motes of golden dust as the sun broke through the clouds.

The dhatura flowers were in bloom, and their heady overpowering smell filled the air. The dhatura plant is deadly and its hallucinatory poison carries both dreams and delusions. The other flowers had been beaten under by the squalls. Pooran had tried to mend his garden, to return order and harmony, but it would take time.

I was wandering around the squelchy, defeated

grass, and maybe it was the season, or the sight of Nina, rescued from death, returning to the shade of the two immortals—I found myself thinking of life, the tangled web of it. Perhaps it was like a spider's web, with its concentric circles and intuitive geometry. There was a pattern to life, in recurrence and circularity, in seashells, in poetry, in the Fibonacci sequence. And yet it was arbitrary and unpredictable.

Badi Amma walked into the garden. She was carrying a book in her hand. 'This is for you,' she said. 'Peter Saheb's book.'

And there it was. *Folk Tales of Kumaon and Garhwal* by Peter Paul Singh. It had a woodcut for a cover, of a woman and a tree. I turned the pages. There was a frontispiece. It was the unsigned painting, the painting in the library. The painting of my grandmother, with her faceless strength.

It was difficult to read the small print in the mildewed paper. 'Frontispiece: EVERYWOMAN. Painting by the author.'

When I turned around to speak to my grandmother, to thank her for this gift, she had gone back inside.

I settled in a corner of the verandah and began reading.

> 'These folk tales, gathered almost a century ago by a Russian linguist and a scholar, reveal the humour, irony and wisdom of oral traditions in the Kumaon region. The voices of Himalayan storytellers—translated from Kumaoni and Hindustani into Russian and German—and now into English—display the universality of human nature. In their seeming simplicity lies great wisdom.'
>
> 'Stories are the outpouring of our fears and hopes, constructs of our imagination,' Peter Paul Singh's introduction continued. 'Folk tales are the collective dreams of a community, its dreaming mind.'

I fell into a reverie. I remembered the stories Badi Amma used to tell me, as dark shadows danced around the rafters of the rooms in Khata Khumani.

All the remembered stories were in the book. I could hear my grandmother's voice in them. The story of the Clever Wife, the Kidnapped Princess, the Banished Prince—these were all familiar territory. They were my childhood.

'She wandered alone in the dark forest. The owls were hooting amidst the overhanging branches. The moon was shining high in the sky, but the forest was darker than the night…'

I longed for my childhood, for the safety and security of my grandmother's stories and her embrace. In her warm embrace I had known pure, complete happiness. Suddenly, I couldn't bear to encounter those stories again. I was sobbing uncontrollably for reasons I could not understand.

> 'There was once a rich and powerful village headman, who had many cows and buffaloes, fields of rice and orchards of fruit. His wife was very beautiful but she had one fault—she mocked everything and everyone, even her husband... One day a fakir came to their village and requested alms and shelter for the night. The headman requested his wife to give the fakir bedding and food. But she was rude to the stranger who was their guest and gave him stale food.
>
> 'The fakir was angered and used his powerful magic to call a witch to humble the proud wife and teach her a lesson. The witch entered the house in the shape of a monkey, a langur. She was accompanied by her apprentice, who came in the form of a raven...'

Just then there was a scream from the garden and I stepped out to check what had happened. As if by some magical synchronicity between the story and its enactment, an enormous langur had actually entered the garden, startling Parvati, and settled itself on one of the garden chairs. Was it the fakir in disguise? Or the witch?

And was that a raven in the mulberry tree?

I took the book upstairs to my room, wrapped it in a scarf and placed it carefully under my pillow. Then I wandered down again.

Sounds of laughter from Nina's bedroom—now Sunita's room as well. I peeped in.

Nina was looking tidier than before. Sunita had braided her hair into two neat plaits which had been doubled over and were looped over her ears. It looked oddly endearing. She was lying in bed, with her plastered leg raised on a pillow. She had a notebook in her hands and was reading something out to Sunita.

I recognised the notebook. 'The Poems of an Immpossible Romantic'

Nina read out a few lines in a sing-song voice.

'The World is a puzzle
Life is a muzzle.
I want to be free
But how can that be?'

She looked up and noticed me by the door.

'What do you think, Iti?' She wasn't wearing lenses today, but her eyes were as startling as ever. 'I'm finally thinking of posting these poems and letting them out into the world now that I am a social media star. What do you think?'

I looked at her closely. I had never heard her laugh before. I thought of the Roerich paintings, and the crude slashes at their edges. Could Nina be trusted again?

I faltered, then pursed my lips. 'Go ahead,' I said simply. 'Post away.'

I shut the door behind me and heard sounds of laughter again. Sunita had begun telling her a story. Nina's laugh had a clear, unassuming tinkle.

I listened quietly, then crept away.

14. WHO LET THE GHOSTS OUT?

That was the afternoon everything changed.

Rosinka was sitting in the verandah. There was a dreamy look in her eyes.

'I dreamt I was a baby again,' she said. 'I wonder if that means I'm going to die.'

'Why would it mean that?' I asked. 'Besides, you are immortal.'

'It's to do with foetal memory,' she said. 'A return to the womb. That is where we all return.'

'What are your first memories?' I asked, wanting her to talk of something else, not her dying.

'Of my Russian grandmother,' Rosinka said unhesitatingly. 'Of her blue eyes. Her smile.'

'I thought you had a Scottish grandmother,' I said.

'Details, details, Iti! Why are you so tiresome? Everyone has at least two grandmothers—sometimes three, as you have me!'

I could see that she was not in the mood to answer questions. Her face was beginning to look tired. A blob of mucous nestled at the edge of her slate-grey eyes. She had used eyeliner today. Who could have helped her apply it? Not Nina, surely. Parvati? Sunita?

'I dreamt of your mother,' Badi Amma said to me as I was leaving the drawing room. 'In the dream, she was speaking to me. She hasn't spoken to me for thirty years. I hope she is all right.'

Late that afternoon, the landline rang. My mother had died in Bangalore. It had been sudden. She had gone in peace.

Her husband—I found it difficult to think of him as my stepfather, considering I hardly knew him—was kind but distant when he conveyed the news. The funeral was that very afternoon. There was no point in my trying to make it there.

I tried to grieve, but the whole thing seemed

incomprehensible. I tried to remember my mother, but the memories, as always, were patchy and for the most part hurtful. I lay in bed with my head under the quilt. Some dry sobs escaped me, but that was all.

Mothers. We are supposed to love them. I never did. My feelings oscillated between indifference, passive hatred, active hatred, and a yearning to be loved by her.

Looking back, now that she is gone, I try to be charitable and ascribe her failings to the unfavourable emotional terrain we inhabited. She was burdened with duties and responsibilities she did not have the capacity to shoulder. She lacked will and a sense of self, which she made up for by assuming a rigid inflexibility. She called this 'discipline', but in fact it had nothing to do with exemplary behaviour or punitive action. It was instead an unsteady and half-hearted effort to assert authority, only because she thought it was expected of her.

What did she think of me, how did she feel about me?

There was a diffidence about the way she spoke to me, a distance which neither of us could ever bridge. Like a dog, I could smell out her fear, and this unleashed a sort of tepid insolence inside me.

Then there was Badi Amma, who was everything a grandmother could be. She mothered me, gave me warmth and affection. She was not afraid of loving me. She was not afraid of love.

When I was young—I can't remember how old—I spent some weeks with my mother in Roorkee. My school was closed for the winter and Rosinka had taken Badi Amma with her to Calcutta for something. I begged my mother to let me have a pet, it would keep me company when she was away at work. She ignored my pleas, took no notice of them. And then, on a rainy morning, we found a tiny kitten by our front door.

'You can keep this little kitty as your pet,' she said casually. 'I like cats. Your grandmother does too, so you can take it back with you.'

We looked after the kitten together, fed it warm milk with a dropper, kept it safe, snuggled in a torn blanket. It was a ginger cat, with a lazy, majestic manner. He grew to rule over us in a gentle happy way. We named him Pussa.

Mother never hugged me—absence of physical warmth and spontaneity characterised our relationship. But she snuggled up to Pussa, played with him, stroked him under the chin and made him purr. She looked different then, her face softened, her shoulders relaxed. I glimpsed there the mother I wished I had.

Now that she is gone, perhaps that is how I should try to remember her, playing with Pussa, making him purr.

It was not that my mother did not try to reach out—she did, furtively, clumsily. But some unspoken wall stood between us always. Neither of us had ever been able to bridge the distance.

And now she was gone. It was as though she had never existed.

'We should go to Bangalore,' Badi Amma said.

'It's too late, Lily,' Rosinka said. 'You are too old, and it's too late to make amends. Bangalore is a long way away. You would have to drive down to Delhi and take a flight.'

'We must go,' Badi Amma persisted.

'I will go to the Café and figure out a taxi and then a flight from Delhi,' I said.

As I stepped out, my phone suddenly came alive. Messages and emails began streaming in. The new Internet tower had become functional. And then it went dead again, like a radio blip from a distant planet.

I thought of my mother, of the smell of her, and how her lips had always drooped at the edges, and the gap between her front teeth. When had the space between us grown so vast? Which of us had given up first?

The café was buzzing with action. A famous cricketer—a pahari from these hills—and his wife had stopped there for a coffee and a toilet break. Avinash was looking harassed but happy. He smiled at me and rushed off. I perched myself near the counter and checked out flight options on my phone. The fares were exorbitantly expensive. We would need to book a hotel too, as her husband, my stepfather, was a virtual stranger.

It seemed strange to be at this physical and emotional distance from the person who had given me birth. Had she thought of me before she died? Or of her mother? What was she fleeing from? Where had she fled?

Pooran arrived at the Café just then. 'Rosinka Madame is unwell!' he said. 'The doctor is there. I'm going to get some medicines.'

I ran up the hill. My heart was pounding. Tears were streaming down my cheeks. It was Rosinka who had held my life together. I could not let her go.

I had not shed any tears for my mother so far. These tears were for her too, and for my distant childhood. As I neared the gates of The Dacha, I tripped over the exposed roots of a tree that had treacherously reached out to entrap me. I bruised my arms and scraped my knees, and when I tried to get up, I found my ankles were no longer holding me up. I crawled into the garden and cried out for help.

Parvati came out and aided me. There was a lady doctor sitting in the verandah, with a stethoscope around her neck. She was drinking tea. A tall untidy man stood beside her, holding a large, shabby doctor's bag. She got up when she saw me and helped me hobble inside. 'What have you done to yourself?' she asked, in the most musical voice I had ever heard. Perhaps she was an angel, I thought confusedly, before I fainted.

It was a blur after that. The tall man carried me inside. When I came to, I was lying on the drawing-room sofa. 'Where's Rosinka?' I remembered crying. 'Is she dead!'

Rosinka's laughter echoed across the room. 'I won't depart so easily,' she declared. 'Just decided to give everybody a scare—but you and your dear departed mother upstaged me.'

Badi Amma was weeping. Nina had limped out of her room to join in the drama. It felt like the last act of a comedy, except that my mother had just died. But Rosinka was still alive. My eyes stung with tears of relief.

'Dr Reddy, this is my daughter, Iti,' Rosinka said.

'Iti, this is Dr Reddy, our new neighbour,' she continued. 'I've told you about her.'

I gave up making sense of things. Dr Reddy gave me a glass of water to drink. She felt my pulse. She checked out things with her stethoscope. She took my temperature. She gave me some pills to swallow and wrapped a crepe bandage around my ankles and calves.

'Right as rain,' she said, in her tinkling voice.

'Rain isn't right,' I replied.

She responded with a musical laugh. 'Nevertheless, a remarkable recovery…' she said. 'I've only recently retired as a paediatrician, but I can look after all ages. I'm delighted to meet you charming ladies, and shall drop in twice a week to check things out. Until then—be good.'

And she left, with the tall man trailing after her.

'We, the living,' Rosinka said triumphantly.

She continued thoughtfully, 'We, the Living. The greatest classic of world literature. I've read it twice. I wish you could read it, Lily, but I don't suppose it has been translated into Hindi.'

She turned to Nina. 'It's written by Andy—no, Annie. Annie Rand. You should read it sometime. It will teach you a thing or two.'

'I will,' Nina replied. 'I surely will.' She seemed as relieved and happy as the rest of us that Rosinka was alive.

'What happened to Rosinka?' I asked Badi Amma.

'She felt dizzy and fell down. Her face lost colour. She

couldn't speak. Pooran called in our new neighbour, Dr Reddy. Madam used to have fainting fits when she was young but she has been so fit all these years.'

I noted that she had reverted to calling her 'Madam' instead of Rosinka. It had been a strange day.

'Why did she call me her daughter?' I asked.

Badi Amma sighed. 'Maybe she was confused. I've noticed that her mind is wandering these days. She is older than me, though she seems younger. Age catches up with everyone. Even her.'

'We are not going to Bangalore,' I told Badi Amma. 'We will go nowhere.'

Badi Amma smiled. 'We are not immortal,' she said. 'We don't have amrit for breakfast. Our time is fast approaching. You are still young. You have your life ahead of you.'

'You are immortal,' I said, hugging her.

15. THE LAST ROSE OF SUMMER

The setting: the sitting room at The Dacha. The mood: nostalgic. Late evening. The weather: balmy, but with a hint of approaching winter. Dramatis Personae: Rosinka, Badi Amma and yours truly.

Rosinka had instructed Badi Amma to light up some candles. There were four tall creamy pillars, edged and laced with ancient wax. They smelt of musty roses and gave off a golden glow.

And the flowers. There was a young magnolia bud, and a mature drooping magnolia beside it, with the spirally yellow stamens clustered around the languid petals.

'I am in the mood for music,' Rosinka announced grandly. 'But first—let us raise a toast. To friends, to family, to loved ones.'

She tottered off to the cabinet and poured the red wine into rather dusty-looking goblets. 'We shall all raise a toast together! And Lily will drink some wine too. No saying no, my friend.'

Badi Amma looked wary. We sat down together. The wine was superb.

There was an old gramophone player which had been brought out from god knows where and placed on a side table. To my utter surprise, Rosinka managed to crank it up and get it going.

Music filled the air. It had begun drizzling and there was a gentle pitter-patter on the tin roof. It was magical.

'Tis the last rose of Summer
Left blooming all alone;
All her lovely companions
Are faded and gone;
No flower of her kindred,
No rose-bud is nigh,
To reflect back her blushes
Or give sigh for sigh…

As if on cue, the music ground to a halt—but somehow still continued to echo through the room.

'The machine has given up on us!' Rosinka said. 'One should never trust machines. I have the music here before me, and the words.'

It had clearly been an act of will or sorcery on Rosinka's part to get the old gramophone going. Or an illusion. Now she began singing, in a quavering but confident voice.

So soon may I follow
When friendships decay
And from Love's shining circle
The gems drop away!

She turned to me. 'Iti, some more wine please—for all of us.'

I did as I was told, compliantly, submissively. I was in her thrall.

When true hearts lie withered
And fond ones are flown,
Oh! Who would inhabit
This bleak world alone?

I was weeping. Salty tears were coursing down my cheeks. I loved her, I loved Rosinka, for all that she was, in spite of all that she was.

'It's an old Irish song,' she said, 'but I remember it from that film... I forget the name.'

The song haunted me that night, even as the owls hooted outside and the rafters creaked: 'The Last Rose of Summer'.

16. DIGITAL DAYS

The Internet has arrived at The Dacha. I don't access it much—I've got out of the habit, and the connectivity is consistently patchy in any case. It intrudes. But it also confirms the world that is waiting at our doorsteps.

I've begun working on a new novel, abandoning all the earlier unfinished ones. A story is emerging, but stories tend to get confused with other stories. A straight narrative with a clear arc of actions and consequences is clearly not possible. Especially not here, in Never Never Land.

Autumn has arrived and dug its heels in. The trees

have changed colour. Red and yellow everywhere. The night sky is clear. The days are awash with brilliant sunshine. The evenings are cold but tender.

It has snowed in the high Himalaya. The familiar peaks greet me every morning, before the cloud line begins to veil them.

The magpie watches over me as I sit in the garden and read from the book of folk tales that Peter Paul Singh translated into English from the German. Or was it from the Russian version? Stories circle like the murmuration of birds in the sky, so many of them, and yet, often, the same stories.

There was a story Badi Amma used to tell me, of the girl who lived with her ancient grandmother in Never Never Land. I searched for the story in Peter's book, but couldn't find it.

There was another story that Badi Amma would tell me, about a snow-white crow that would dance across the sky in the high mountains when winter announced itself. It was the harbinger of a harsh and bitter winter, that bird, of snowstorms and avalanches, and people would tremble with fear when they saw it. That story was in the book. I read and re-read it.

Crows and ravens and magpies, they are all corvids,

clever and astute. They can recognise faces and hold a grudge. They can make tools and hide their food. They mate for life. They have funerals for their dead.

I dreamt of a white raven, but then it became a magpie, my magpie, and flew away. Owls hooted all night. Dogs howled and bayed at the moon. Moths fluttered behind thin curtains.

The weather has changed again. Rain and hail and sleet for days on end. A helicopter has crashed near Badrinath. Buses have disappeared into ravines and khuds and rivers are in spate. The electricity comes and goes. The Internet keeps us alerted and updated to the havoc around. They call it climate change and global warming and sterile words like that, but it is more than that. It is the wrath of the gods.

That is what Badi Amma told me, and I believe her. 'Uttaranchal, our Uttarakhand, is the Dev Bhoomi, the land of the Gods. That is what they call it in the Manas Khand, in the ancient epics. Now, the Mountain Gods are impatient beings—they like solitude, they don't enjoy being jostled around. So they have decided to push away the tourists and the greedy builders who are polluting our Dev Bhoomi. They will push them over the cliffs, they will bury them under landslides, they will drown them in the overflowing rivers.'

'If they still don't understand,' she added, 'they will set the forests on fire. They will reclaim our sacred land and make it green and young again.'

I had never seen her so passionate about anything before.

She was not the only one. Pooran and his wife Parvati returned from the temple in the next village whispering to each other. They looked troubled.

'What's the matter? You look worried,' I said to Parvati.

Pooran replied on her behalf. 'A holy man had come from high in the Himalaya to visit the temple in the next village,' he said. 'He told us the Gods are going to depart from these mountains until humans mend their ways. They will send ghouls and spirits to drive the humans away. A noble bear will be crowned King and rule over hill and dale. Only seekers and righteous people shall be allowed here—the rest will be tipped back like garbage to the plains below. It has happened in Joshimath already, the sadhu said, and it will happen everywhere.'

It sounded dire, but also reassuring, depending on the perspective from which you examined prophecies.

Now Parvati took over from Pooran. 'We had heard of Shivji's Tandava—now we shall witness Devi Bhairavi's dance of destruction! The Goddesses will not go away—they will guard the secrets until the Gods return.'

It sounded confusing but somehow comforting. Parvati looked at her watch. 'I have to marinate the lamb chops,' she said, 'and make khichdi for Badi Amma! The Gods will not descend to help me in the kitchen!'

I'm working away steadily at my novel. I've written by candlelight through some of these dark and apocalyptic nights. Sunita watches over the ladies.

I was once briefly mentored by a well-known writing coach. The lady reprimanded me for my excessive use of poetry and long quotations. 'It is a sign of inadequacy, a symptom of your lack of originality and creativity,' she had said smugly. She liked putting me down, it was clearly one of the perks and rewards of her job.

My question is this—if something makes me feel less unfinished, less muddled by effectively and more adequately evoking the sentiments I'm trying to evoke, why should it be dissed by these supposedly superior beings? I didn't say it to her then, but I would if I were to meet her again.

My phone with its reassuring torch is my friend and companion. The rain beating on the roof has entered my bloodstream, and become a part of the rhythm of my prose.

Something has shifted gear inside me through these monsoon months in The Dacha. I'm no longer trying to belong, to be accepted, to merge with the larger colour scheme.

I returned after a long gap to scan the school WhatsApp group. They are a sweet bunch of aging girls, cheering each other on as they share games and life lessons and inspirational quotes and giggles. They are kind and comfortable with each other, secure in their lives, attuned to their expectations.

I wish I could be more like them—I confess that I do—but somewhere I remain the awkward outsider in that constant cheerful chatter. I don't want to try; I don't want to fail. I'm beginning to feel this half-life is easier to live than theirs.

I considered putting up a photo of myself standing in the garden of The Dacha, swathed in mist and mystery, and announcing that I was on a sabbatical, writing my much-awaited novel—but then, nobody seemed to have even noticed my absence...

One of the girls in the group put up a somber post. 'Remember Anita Shivdasani? She had died by suicide, all those years ago. She used to wear spectacles with red frames and had two long plaits.' (This was accompanied by a heartbreak emoji.)

'Well, Anita Shivdasani's mom was my aunt Aruna's neighbour in Denver. She died last week in a mass shooting in a supermarket there. RIP Aunty Shivdasani. Hope you meet Anita in your journey to heaven. Om Shanti.'

My heart stopped, it skipped several beats before it began pumping again. I had forgotten about the red spectacles. My friend Anita. She too had carried a pool of loneliness within her, which had pushed her to leave us.

There were some likes and some teary responses before the herd moved on to holiday snapshots. Corfu. Cincinnati. Chennai.

I knew I had to do it then. The time had come to exit the group. My fingers tapped nervously on the screen as I typed out a terse farewell. 'I am leaving you all for personal reasons. Take care girls and stay well. Until we meet again. Yours, Iti Arya.'

I don't know what happened after that, whether anybody noticed my departure or bothered to comment about it.

Never Never Land. I was alone, and myself, in a place where I belonged. Sometimes we have to retreat to return.

I had got a new pair of spectacles from Haldwani, from a stylish optician who had recently opened shop. 'These tortoise-shell frames will complement your skin tone perfectly,' he had told me, in a voice that did not even try to sound sincere. But I loved the look and feel of them, the round rims, the variegated black-and-yellow frame, so I had succumbed, and paid more than I should have.

I had also changed the power of the lens on his advice. Everything suddenly looked sharper, clearer, magnified.

I wore the new spectacles the evening we were celebrating Rosinka's birthday. She was coy about dates and years. 'I feel young one day and old the other,' she said. 'My age oscillates.'

I had bought eighty candles and a large low square cake that managed to accommodate seventy-three of them.

We had assembled a small party. Pooran and Parvati

had been asked to join us in the drawing room. Dr Reddy had come too. And there were Nina and Sunita, Badi Amma and me. And Rosinka.

She wore a pink cashmere shawl embellished with pearls and beadwork and a lace trim which smelt of mothballs. She had matched her nail polish to the exact deep flamingo pink of the shawl. She had chosen mauve eye shadow for the event. Her eyes sparkled.

Badi Amma had a bit of stringy mucous lodged in the corner of one eye. She was wearing her patient expression, which meant she wasn't enjoying herself. I felt fiercely protective of her. I wanted to wipe the goo from her eye. I wanted to smooth her brow.

But Rosinka demanded a glass of wine. Badi Amma smiled indulgently and waddled off to the bar.

We raised a toast. Rosinka commanded us to blow out the candles. 'I don't want to get out of breath...' she said. We huffed and we puffed. We raised a toast. We sang Happy Birthday.

The wax from the tiny candles had splattered over the cake. It tasted strange. One lone candle persisted in the midst of the massacre.

'I'm tired,' Rosinka said tremulously. 'Goodnight, sweet friends.'

I felt a sense of dread. They were old. They were fragile. I never wanted to let them go.

And now the rain has stopped, and the sun is out again. The eternal snows of Nanda Devi and Chaukhumba and Panchachuli smile down upon us.

There are so many smells in the air, of leaves and flowers and rain and rotting vegetation. It is not renewal, but revival.

And then this too will pass, and the tattered cycle of the seasons will reassert itself. The poinsettias will bloom, and then the rhododendrons. There will be mulberries and kaphal berries and then the strawberries will arrive with the summer.

There is a row of first edition books by Rudyard Kipling I found in the damp bookcase in the study. They must be valuable. I've put them out to dry, agitating the silver fish that had made their home between the covers.

Kipling is out of fashion, but there are some lines I have always loved. They go something like this:

> *... and the last puff of the day brought from the unseen villages the scent of damp wood-smoke, hot cakes,*

dripping undergrowth, and rotting pine cones. That is the true smell of the Himalayas, and once it creeps into the blood of a man, that man will at the last, forgetting all else, return to the hills to die.

It will be a long cold winter. But we will all carry on. Me, us, these mountains.

CODA

NETTLE SOUP

(Recipe by Lily. Tasted, approved and recorded by Rosinka Paul Singh. January 9th, 1956)

There are many sorts of stinging nettle leaves—for example, 'ghariye shishuna', 'patle shishuna', and 'bhangrey shishuna'.

It is also known in Kumaon as Bichhu Patta, or Scorpion Grass.

Cooking instructions:

- Pluck the tops of the green shishuna leaves. Be careful while washing them and never use plastic gloves as they can embed in the plastic and hurt your skin.
- Heat some oil (preferably mustard oil) in a broad pot. Put in the leaves and some water and let them simmer. Cook them as you would cook spinach leaves, except that you have to be more careful, as spinach leaves don't bite! After braising the nettle leaves, pour more water and let it come to a boil.
- Separately, take some vegetables, such as carrots or potatoes, dice and fry them lightly in butter or ghee, and add water. Bring to the boil, then add the vegetables to the pot of boiling nettles. Mash them with a large spoon and season to taste with salt and dhaniya (coriander) powder. There is no need to add any chillies or chilli powder.

Nettle leaves are rich in protein and minerals and are a good source of vitamins.

Gratitude

To Aishwarya Dani for helping hold the book together through its various stages.

Thank you, Ravi Singh and everyone at Speaking Tiger.

And thank you Hemali Sodhi, John Curzon, and all those who believe in fictional worlds.

ALSO FROM SPEAKING TIGER

HIMALAYA

Adventures, Meditations, Life

Edited by Ruskin Bond and Namita Gokhale

'Eclectic pickings you may otherwise encounter in a lifetime of reading... [This anthology] is a delicious hoard.'—*India Today*

With over forty essays, this comprehensive volume brings together a dazzling range of voices—of explorers, ascetics, climbers, caravaneers and spies, among others—from Fa-Hein, Jahangir and Vivekananda to Edmund Hillary, Peter Matheissen and Manjushree Thapa. Here you will find stories of great ascents and descents; grand epiphanies and life-changing visions; tales of exploratory derring-do; and a mutiny up on a mountain.

A seeker has an intense spiritual experience on Mount Kailas, another among shamans on a mountaintop in Nepal; and, looking for the snow leopard in Ladakh, an author finds himself. A resident of a Sherpa village writes of the aftermath of an avalanche which killed porters and climbers on Everest; and residents of Langtang record an oral history of the earthquake which wiped out their village. A matriarch describes her life and family in Almora of a bygone time; and the fragrance of lime makes a traveller's night in a remote Garhwal village memorable for all time.

Edited by Ruskin Bond, India's most-loved writer, and acclaimed novelist Namita Gokhale, this anthology spans the entire range of the Himalaya, from the foothills to the highest peaks, and from its easternmost to its westernmost ends. It will keep you riveted.